*Colonialism and
Gender Relations
from
Mary Wollstonecraft
to Jamaica Kincaid*

Colonialism and Gender Relations from Mary Wollstonecraft to Jamaica Kincaid

EAST CARIBBEAN CONNECTIONS

Moira Ferguson

COLUMBIA UNIVERSITY PRESS

NEW YORK

Columbia University Press
New York   Chichester, West Sussex

Copyright © 1993 Columbia University Press
All rights reserved

Library of Congress Cataloging-in-Publication Data

Ferguson, Moira.
  Colonial and gender relations from Mary Wollstonecraft to Jamaica
Kincaid : East Caribbean connections / Moira Ferguson.
      p.   cm.
  Includes bibliographical references and index.
  ISBN: 978-0-231-08223-5 (pbk.: alk. paper)
  1. English literature—Caribbean influences.   2. English literature—
Women authors—History and criticism.   3. Women and literature—
Caribbean Area—History.   4. Women and literature—Great Britain—
History.   5. Slavery and slaves in literature.   6. Caribbean Area in
literature.   7. Race relations in literature.   8. Imperialism in literature.
9. Colonies in literature.   10. Sex role in literature.   I. Title.
PR129.C37F47   1993
820.9′9287—dc20   92–39302
                                                                          CIP

For Gillian

Contents

Acknowledgments

I have incurred many personal and professional debts in the course of writing this book. I am grateful to the University of Sussex; the Inter-University Centre of Postgraduate Studies, Dubrovnik, Yugoslavia; Pennsylvania State University; St. Mary's College, Notre Dame, Indiana; The Minority Literature Group, Lincoln, Nebraska; and the Modern Language Association for inviting me to present my research on colonial and gender relations. The chapters on Mary Wollstonecraft and *Mansfield Park* originally appeared in slightly different form in the *Feminist Review* and the *Oxford Literary Review*. I thank the editors warmly. Many thanks, too, to Jennifer Crewe and Anne McCoy of Columbia University Press, for invaluable assistance and support. I am also grateful to Roma Rector for typing the manuscript with her customary finesse and to research assistants Kate Flaherty, Nicolle French, Xiaofei Tian, Lisa Toay, and Lisa Weems for fine assistance. I also thank students in several eighteenth-century and modern fiction courses and seminars.

Acknowledgments

For valuable readings of individual chapters, I thank Nora Gaines, Cora Kaplan, Franklin Knight, Irma Nippert, Robert Young, and the *Feminist Review* Collective. For incisive readings of the manuscript in its final draft, I owe a special debt to Elizabeth Fox-Genovese and Ketu Katrak.

Colonialism and
Gender Relations
from
Mary Wollstonecraft
to Jamaica Kincaid

Introduction

In this book I examine connections between gender and colonial
relations in texts by British writers of the eighteenth and nineteenth centuries and Caribbean writers of the nineteenth and twen-
tieth centuries: Mary Wollstonecraft, Anne Hart Gilbert, Elizabeth
Hart Thwaites, Jane Austen, Jean Rhys, and Jamaica Kincaid. I
argue that these women writers were bound by their participation
in a discourse about East Caribbean and British women and African-Caribbean slaves, which they were determined to extend and
amplify to fit different situations at the metropolitan center and its
periphery. Their relations to this discourse varied significantly,
however, according to situation and cultural context and the specific political and spiritual goals that these authors had in mind.
The text suggests, moreover, that focusing on the specific colonial situation permitted women to see and say things—especially
in the sexual arena—that they might not otherwise have seen and
said.

In other words I analyze how the writings themselves dialogically
interrelate. Using the historical backdrop of slavery and colonial-

1

ism, the text investigates how white and African-Caribbean women writers configure feminist, abolitionist, and post-emancipationist agendas. How are texts articulated differently according to locale and the author's relationship to the colonial order? What role does cultural context play?

There are at least two major points of departure for the study. The first is a discrete area of the East Caribbean, the island of Antigua. Throughout the women's texts, Antigua is a critical site of textual and historical contestation where opposition to white male control of a predominantly African-Caribbean population plays itself out. The Hart sisters live in Antigua; Sir Thomas Bertram's fictional estate is there and he visits the island, while Jamaica Kincaid was born and raised in Antigua. Dominica, Antigua's neighbor to the south, is the setting for *Wide Sargasso Sea*. In addition it is the island from which the maternal side of Jamaica Kincaid's family comes, her grandmother having been one of the few remaining Carib Indians. Furthermore, this contrast of British and Antiguan authors underscores epistemological differences, how white women, free women of color, and slaves discern their respective situations. The second common point of departure is the complex textual embedding of imposed sexuality as a sign of domination.

The study begins with a discussion of Mary Wollstonecraft's struggle for white middle-class women's rights in the metropolitan center and her constant recourse to slavery as an analogy when she discusses these rights; that is, slavery and its referents signal tyranny in *A Vindication of the Rights of Woman*. Introducing the thematic of colonial and gender relations in tandem, possibly the first woman to do so at a theoretical level, Wollstonecraft demonstrates in the *The Rights of Woman* how the abolitionist movement facilitated the scrutiny of women's rights. Deliberating on white women's resentment of their powerlessness, Wollstonecraft persistently links colonial slavery to female subjugation and male desire; she exposes connections between sexual and political power, using sexuality to suggest overlappings between the oppression of white women and black women slaves. I further argue that in Wollstonecraft's text, liberating ideas push up through the text and dialogically refute the hegemonic, self-contradictory discourse of bourgeois feminism.

Just as defiant and ground-breaking as Mary Wollstonecraft, though in a very different cultural context, Anne Hart Gilbert and Elizabeth Hart Thwaites engage the struggle for rights in Antigua, a site at the margins of the colonial nexus. Just as much if not more to the point, where Mary Wollstonecraft casts homogeneously conceived Africans as inferior according to received white dictates of the day, the Hart sisters insist on human equality conceived heterogeneously. Their role as religious educators offers them an important status and a public voice in Antigua and simultaneously allows them a cover of sorts for abolitionist and emancipationist activities. Their questioning of the condition of slaves, particularly female slaves, is a positive political act in its own right and a way of opening up discourse about the general condition of African-Caribbeans in Antigua and their own complex standing as relatively well-known free women of color or, in the official designation, "free-colored" females. In other words religion functions as social coding in pre-emancipation Antiguan society in which racial tensions are high and agitation threatens the endangered ruling class. The fact that the sisters write before and after the passage of the Abolition Bill in 1807 and up to the Emancipation Bill in 1833 further complicates their texts. So does their subtle campaign against an image of black women linked to sexuality and degradation. They also use a spiritually condoned discourse on the rights of female slaves to promote literacy and oppose physical violation—a variant of Wollstonecraft's demands in a fundamentally different context.

Of added interest in the case of the Hart sisters is the slippage between their own necessarily mediated discourse and that of white commentators who wrote about them. Their eulogists, for example, saw what they wanted to see. In that sense the writings of the Hart sisters generate multiple contexts that sharpen their differences from novels and polemic written by authors at the heart of the colonial empire.

Introduction

In *Mansfield Park* Jane Austen again foregrounds Antigua because of personal knowledge about her family's participation in plantation-owning class relations on that island. What's more, unlike the texts of the Hart sisters where gender and colonial relations are inextricably connected and sometimes even fused, the novel presents gender relations at home that parallel and echo traditional relations of power between colonialists and colonized people. Slavery, then, is central to *Mansfield Park* yet ambiguously so, because Austen is primarily concerned with the refiguring of a legitimate British ruling class in the wake of the French Revolution and in the emergence of a newly aggressive capitalism.

Written about a period of Antiguan and British history roughly comparable to the sisters' texts, *Mansfield Park* avows the importance of vantage points and cultural context. Austen writes from the "mother country" about a restless colony. The Hart sisters, by contrast, talk about direct experiences in that colony and how iniquities perpetrated there by the British affect all strata of society; these respective texts call and respond to each other indirectly but in opposition. Mary Wollstonecraft and Jane Austen converse somewhat differently, treating similar themes in variant ways, but perhaps with less obvious confrontation. Mary Wollstonecraft's overt recognition of the resemblances between slaves and white British women and Jane Austen's nuanced suggestions about those similarities reflect their political differences, especially their diverse responses to the San Domingo and French revolutions.

Wide Sargasso Sea by Jean Rhys takes place a decade later in fictional time from the texts of the Hart sisters and *Mansfield Park*. Configuring a second East Caribbean scenario from yet another perspective, Rhys discusses a changing colonial, soon to be post-emancipation, situation. Whites are combating not just the victory in San Domingo but a recently freed and incensed population. Conversing at a slant with the Hart sisters' relatively understated texts, *Wide Sargasso Sea* subtly campaigns against the treatment of Antoinette, a representative white creole whose sexuality marks her exchange value in marriage and signals an enforced degradation.

By centerstaging the narrative of an alienated white female estate-owner who has become an object of prey at the hands of a dispossessed metropolitan and colonial white patriarchy, Rhys inverts the view of the Hart sisters on Caribbean society. The roles of insiders and outsiders have become blurred. Rhys links the politics of emancipation with opposition to old and new plantocrats by cross-class, cross-race women who are eventually bonded only by displays of anger executed very differently.

At one important level, then, *Wide Sargasso Sea* bears witness to the conflict between old and new colonizers through the sign of barterable women. However, despite the fact that white characters are a major focus—or so it seems—the African-Caribbean population refuses to be suppressed. The powerful obeah woman Christophine, for example, anchors the text; she is the representative woman from whom the Hart sisters spiritually, though not politically, separate themselves. Christophine underscores the need and desire for unity among those African-Caribbeans who maintain African cultural practices and others who envisage integration within the new order. Historicizing the plantocracy in an epoch of post-emancipation reprisals, Rhys exposes British attempts (through the character of "Rochester") to construct a nouveau plantocracy and the successful challenge from the black population, now legally freed, to thwart these efforts. Denied even the colonizer's script, Rochester finds his authority disintegrating.

After a chronological lapse of several decades, Jamaica Kincaid represents another phase in Antigua's engagement with colonialism and postcolonialism during a shifting balance of power. She writes in the 1980s about Antigua in the 1950s, when the island had attained partial but not full independence from Britain. Mediated through a version of the "real life" relationship with her mother and imbricated with the trials of growing up female in a colonized country, Kincaid emphasizes the arc of the imperial machine that

5

extends back to Christopher Columbus and the start of British colonialism and then joins up with the present day. In that sense *Annie John* and *A Small Place* encompass and intertextualize the ongoing debate from Wollstonecraft and the Hart sisters up to Jane Austen and Jean Rhys.

In pre-independence Antigua Jamaica Kincaid depicts Annie John as a subject who refuses obliteration as an ignorant and presumptuous colonized female object. Ventriloquized through Annie John, Jamaica Kincaid's fight against marginality imposed by race, class, and gender draws into sharp focus the multiple issues raised by Mary Wollstonecraft, Anne Hart Gilbert, Elizabeth Hart Thwaites, Jane Austen, and Jean Rhys; the diverse forms of combat waged by Fanny Price and Antoinette against related marginalities parallel and contest the opposition mounted by Annie John against her containment at all levels. Moreover, by juxtaposing *Annie John* with the postcolonial polemic against Antigua entitled *A Small Place*, Kincaid provocatively suggests how colonization, as well as gender, might have conditioned or constructed Annie John.

This volume, then, traces the gradual emergence of a discourse that focuses on the struggle for rights among activists and commentators at the metropolitan centers and those who wage their assault at the political periphery. In a sense each text is accompanied by the texts that precede it. Allusive presences and embedded oppositions matter; they render all texts as sites of exchange. Writing from various geographic sites at different times on related topics, this diverse sextet collectively affirms that no direct access to the past exists without authorial mediation. How authors see events is how they try to record them. But despite their self-conscious articulations of "how things are," textual eruptions frequently occur. Nonetheless, despite widely varying stances—those who think slaves are irrational versus those who view slaves as men, women, and children brutalized by their environment but always self-determining—these collective acts of writing are transgressive in the context of the times.

From Mary Wollstonecraft and the Hart sisters to Jane Austen,

Jean Rhys, and Jamaica Kincaid, writers allude to and articulate a discourse about gender and colonial relations produced under determinate conditions. This discourse, moreover, is always evolving, sometimes reaching a series of temporary closures, then reopening itself to new possibilities. Within this discourse representations of sexual victimization and self-determination shift according to cultural context.

In some cases women without political allies or a sense of independence become bogged down by historical circumstances and patriarchal stipulations. In other cases—the Hart sisters and Annie John are perhaps the best examples—women transgress the restrictions of a prescribed femininity. Put another way, women who are habitually suppressed retaliate against erasure with fluid, creative strategies.

In their discussions of the ways in which representations of black and white women are both different and similar, these six writers reveal the crucial role played by place, time, sexuality, and cultural positionality in fostering critical intersections of race, class, and gender. The continuum of their writings further suggests that during 150 years of slavery, emancipation, and postcolonialism, recognition of the link between gender and colonial relations became commensurately more clear.

Mary Wollstonecraft
and the Problematic
of Slavery

A traffic that outrages every suggestion of reason and religion . . . [an] inhuman custom.
                            —Mary Wollstonecraft,
        A Vindication of the Rights of Men, p. 24

I love most people best when they are in
adversity, for pity is one of my prevailing
passions.   —*Collected Letters of
                Mary Wollstonecraft*, p. 92

History and Texts Before A Vindication
of the Rights of Woman

In 1790 Mary Wollstonecraft became a major polemicist for the
first time because of her evolving political analysis and social milieu. In contrast to A *Vindication of the Rights of Men* in 1790, which
drew primarily on the language of natural rights for its argument, A

Vindication of the Rights of Woman (1792) favored a discourse on slavery that foregrounded female subjugation. Whereas *The Rights of Men* refers to slavery in a variety of contexts only four or five times, *The Rights of Woman* contains more than eighty references; the constituency Wollstonecraft champions—white, middle-class women—is constantly characterized as slaves. By utilizing an antislavery discourse to talk about white women's rights, Wollstonecraft underscores epistemological differences, how white women and slaves discern their situations differently and how she connects them. For her major polemic Mary Wollstonecraft decided to adopt and adapt the terms of contemporary political debate. Over a two-year period that debate had gradually reformulated its terms as the French Revolution in 1789, which highlighted aristocratic hegemony and bourgeois rights, was followed by the San Domingo Revolution, which focused primarily on colonial relations.[1]

Wollstonecraft's evolving commentaries on the status of European women in relation to slavery were made in response to four interlocking activities and events: first, intense agitation over the question of slavery in England, which included the case of the slave James Somerset in 1772 and Phillis Wheatley's visit in 1773; second, the French Revolution in 1789; third, Catharine Macaulay's *Letters on Education* (1790), which argued forthrightly against sexual difference; and fourth, the successful revolution by slaves in the French colony of San Domingo in 1791.

Wollstonecraft's discourse on slavery was nothing new for women writers, although it was now distinctly recontextualized in terms of colonial slavery. Formerly, in all forms of discourse throughout the eighteenth century, conservative and radical women alike railed against marriage, love, and education as forms of slavery perpetrated upon women by men and by the conventions of society at large.

Before the French Revolution Mary Wollstonecraft had appropriated the language of slavery in texts from various genres. In *Thoughts* (1787), an educational treatise written in 1786, Woll-

9

stonecraft talked conventionally of women subjugated by their husbands who in turn tyrannize servants, "for slavish fear and tyranny
go together."[2] In *Mary, A Fiction* (1788), her first novel written in
Ireland during trying circumstances as a governess, the heroine
decides she will not live with her husband and exclaims to her
family: "I will work . . . , do anything rather than be a slave."[3] As
a case in point, here Wollstonecraft inflects slavery with the orthodox conception of slavery that had populated women's texts for
more than a century—marriage was a form of slavery; wives were
slaves to husbands.

Wollstonecraft's early conventional usage, however, in which
the word *slave* stands for a subjugated daughter or wife, was soon to
complicate its meaning. From the early 1770s onward a number of
events—from James Somerset's court case to Quaker petitions to
Parliament and reports of abuses—had injected the discourse of
slavery into popular public debate.

The Abolition Committee, for example, was formed on May 22,
1787, with a view to mounting a national campaign against the
slave trade and securing the passage of an abolition bill through
Parliament.[4] Following the establishment of the committee, abolitionist Thomas Clarkson wrote and distributed two thousand copies
of a pamphlet entitled "A Summary View of the Slave-Trade, and
of the Probable Consequences of Its Abolition."[5] Wollstonecraft's
friend William Roscoe offered the profits of his poem, "The Wrongs
of Africa," to the committee. The political campaign was launched
on the public in full force.[6]

Less than a year after the Abolition Committee was formed,
Wollstonecraft's radical publisher, Joseph Johnson, cofounded a
radical periodical entitled the *Analytical Review*. Invited to become
a reviewer, Wollstonecraft soon reflected the new influence of the
abolition debate.[7] One of the earliest books she critiqued, in April
1789, was written by Britain's most renowned African and a former
slave. For the first time Wollstonecraft was analyzing a text based
on specific experiences of colonial slavery, and her subscription to
received ideas about Africans was transparent, a point to which I

shall return. Its title was *The Interesting Narrative of the Life of Olaudah Equiano, or Gustavus Vassa, the African. Written by Himself,* in which Equiano graphically chronicles being kidnapped from Africa, launched on the notorious Middle Passage, and living out as a slave the consequences of these events.[8]

While the *Analytical Review* acquainted the public with old and new texts on the current debate, Wollstonecraft was composing an anthology for educating young women that also reflected her growing concerns. Published by Joseph Johnson and entitled *The Female Reader; Or Miscellaneous Pieces for the Improvement of Young Women,* the textbook-cum-anthology included substantial extracts promoting abolition.[9] It included Sir Richard Steele's rendition from the *Spectator* of the legend of Inkle and Yarico, Anna Laetitia Barbauld's hymn-in-prose, "Negro Woman," about a grieving mother forcibly separated from her child, and a poignant passage from William Cowper's poem, *The Task,* which was popular with the contemporary reading public:

> I would not have a slave to till my ground,
> To carry me, to fan me while I sleep,
> And tremble when I wake, for all the wealth
> That sinews bought and sold have ever earn'd.
> No: dear as freedom is, and in my heart's
> Just estimation priz'd above all price,
> I had much rather be myself the slave,
> And wear the bonds, than fasten them on him.[10]

A rapid series of events that followed continued to have a bearing on the reconstitution of the discourse on slavery. In July 1789 the French Revolution erupted as the Bastille jail was symbolically stormed and opened. Coinciding with the French Revolution were Richard Price's polemic, Edmund Burke's response, and then Wollstonecraft's response to Burke and her review of Catharine Macaulay's *Letters on Education.* Meanwhile, in September and the following months, Wollstonecraft reviewed in sections[11] the anti-slavery novel *Zeluco: Various Views of Human Nature, Taken from Life and Manners, Foreign and Domestic* by John Moore. Let me back up and briefly elaborate how all this attentiveness to colonial slavery affected public debate and Mary Wollstonecraft's gendered usage of the term.

On November 4, 1789, Wollstonecraft's friend, the Reverend Richard Price, Dissenting minister and leading liberal philosopher, delivered to the Revolution Society in London the annual sermon commemorating the "Glorious Revolution" of 1688. The society cherished the ideals of the seventeenth-century revolution and advocated Dissenters' rights. This particular year Dissenters had much to celebrate. Price applauded the French Revolution as the start of a liberal epoch: "After sharing in the benefits of one revolution," declared Price [meaning the British seventeenth-century constitutional revolution], "I have been spared to be a witness to two other Revolutions, both glorious." [12] The written text of Price's sermon, *Discourse on the Love of Our Country*, was reviewed by Wollstonecraft in the *Analytical*'s December issue. A year later, on November 1, 1790, Edmund Burke's *Reflections on the Revolution in France*, which attacked both Price and his sermon, was timed for publication on the anniversary of Price's address. [13] It soon became a topic of public debate. Several responses quickly followed.

As the first writer to challenge Burke's reactionary polemic, Wollstonecraft foregrounded the cultural issue of human rights in her title: *A Vindication of the Rights of Men.* [14] It immediately sold out. Not by political coincidence, she composed this reply while evidence about the slave trade was being presented to the Privy Council during the year after the first extensive parliamentary debate on abolition in May 1789. *The Rights of Men* applauded human rights and justice, excoriated abusive social, religious, and state practices, and attacked Burke for hypocrisy and prejudice. She argued vehemently for a more equitable distribution of wealth and parliamentary representation. By December 4, 1790, Wollstonecraft had revised the first edition, and Johnson rapidly turned out a second one in January 1791.[15]

In *The Rights of Men* Wollstonecraft also frontally condemns institutionalized slavery:

> On what principle Mr. Burke could defend American indepen-
> dence, I cannot conceive; for the whole tenor of his plausible
> arguments settles slavery on an everlasting foundation. Allowing
> his servile reverence for antiquity, and prudent attention to self-
> interest, to have the force which he insists on, the slave trade
> ought never to be abolished; and, because our ignorant forefa-
> thers, not understanding the native dignity of man, sanctioned a
> traffic that outrages every suggestion of reason and religion, we
> are to submit to the inhuman custom, and term an atrocious
> insult to humanity the love of our country, and a proper submis-
> sion to the laws by which our property is secured.[16]

In *The Rights of Men* Wollstonecraft argues explicitly for the first time that no slavery is natural, and all forms of slavery, regardless of context, are human constructions. Her scorching words to Burke about his situating slavery "on an everlasting foundation" sharply distinguishes her discourse from the more orthodox invocations of slavery in *Thoughts* and *Mary*. Contemporary events have begun to mark the debate on slavery in a firm and special way.

Wollstonecraft challenges the legal situation in particular. In *The Rights of Men* she graphically represents slavery as "authorized by law to fasten her fangs on human flesh and . . . eat into the very soul."[17] Although she supports abolition unequivocally, she none-theless considers reason an even more important attribute to possess than physical freedom. "Virtuous men," she comments, can endure "poverty, shame, and even slavery" but not the "loss of reason."[18]

The same month that Wollstonecraft replied to Burke, she fa-vorably reviewed Catharine Macaulay's *Letters on Education*. Ma-caulay's argument against the accepted notion that males and fe-males had distinct sexual characteristics was part of the evolving discourse on human rights that connected class relations to women's rights.[19] Macaulay also expropriated the language of physical bondage and wove it into her political argument. Denouncing discrimination against women throughout society, *Letters* also rails against "the savage barbarism which is now displayed on the sultry shores of Africa."[20] Macaulay takes pains to censure the condition of women "in the east"—in harems, for example—and scorns the fact that men used differences in "corporal strength . . . in the barbarous ages to reduce [women] to a state of abject slavery."[21] Macaulay's historical timing separates her from earlier writers who used this language; by 1790 slavery had assumed multiple meanings, which included the recognition, implied or explicit, of connections between colonial slavery and sexual abuse.

In *The Rights of Men* Wollstonecraft had not exhibited any substantial attention to the question of gender. After she read Macaulay, however, her discourse on gender and rights shifted. Notable, too, as one edition after another of *The Rights of Men* hit the presses, Johnson was concurrently publishing Wollstonecraft's translation of Christian Gotthilf Salzmann's *Elements of Morality for the Use of Children.* In the preface to this educational treatise Wollstonecraft pointedly inserted a passage of her own, enjoining the fair treatment of Native Americans.[22] In terms of democratic colonial relations as they were then perceived, Wollstonecraft rendered Salzmann more up to date. There was, however, still more to come before Wollstonecraft settled into writing her second *The Rights of Woman* in 1792.

First of all, information about slavery continued to flow unabated in the press. According to Michael Craton, "William Wilberforce was able to initiate the series of pioneer inquiries before the Privy Council and select committees of Commons and Lords, which brought something like the truth of slave trade and plantation slavery out into the open between 1789 and 1791."[23] Nonetheless, in April 1791 the Abolition Bill was defeated in the House of Commons by a vote of 163 to 88, a massive blow to the antislavery campaign.

Just as much (if not much more) to the point, in August of that year slaves in the French colony of San Domingo (now Haiti) revolted, another crucial historical turning point. The French Caribbean had been "an integral part of the economic life of the age, the greatest colony in the world, the pride of France, and the envy of every other imperialist nation."[24]

The conjunction of these events deeply polarized British society. George III switched to the proslavery side, enabling faint-hearted abolitionists to change sides. Meanwhile radicals celebrated. The triumphant uprising of the San Domingan slaves forced another angle of vision on the French Revolution and compounded the anxiety that affairs across the Channel had generated. Horrified at the threat to their investments and fearful of copycat insurrections by the domestic working class as well as by African-Caribbeans, many panic-stricken whites denounced the San Domingan revolution.[25]

Although no one spoke their pessimism outright, abolition was temporarily doomed. When campaigners remobilized in 1792, they were confident of winning the vote and refused to face the implications of dual revolutions in France and San Domingo. Now quite sanguine, proslaveryites capitalized on the intense conflicts and instigated a successful policy of delay. A motion for gradual abolition—effectively a plantocratic victory—carried in the Commons by a vote of 238 to 85.

A Vindication of the Rights of Woman

The composition of A *Vindication of the Rights of Woman* started in the midst of these tumultuous events, its political ingredients indicating Wollstonecraft's involvement in all the issues. Indeed Mary Wollstonecraft seems to have been the first writer to raise issues of colonial and gender relations so tellingly in tandem.

More than any previous text, *The Rights of Woman* invokes the language of colonial slavery to impugn female subjugation and call for the restoration of inherent rights. Wollstonecraft's eighty-plus references to slavery divide into several categories and subsets. The language of slavery—unspecified—is attached to sensation, pleasure, fashion, marriage, and patriarchal subjugation. It is also occasionally attached to the specific condition of colonized slaves.

Wollstonecraft starts from the premise that all men enslave all women and that sexual desire is a primary motivation: "I view, with indignation, the mistaken notions that enslave my sex. . . . For I will venture to assert, that all the causes of female weakness, as well as depravity, which I have already enlarged on, branch out of one grand cause—want of chastity in men."[26]

Men dominate women as plantocrats dominate slaves. "As blind obedience is ever sought for by power, tyrants and sensualists are in the right when they endeavour to keep women in the dark, because the former only want slaves and the latter a play-thing. . . . All the sacred rights of humanity are violated by insisting on blind obedience; or, the most sacred rights belong *only* to man" (pp. 44 and 83). In permeating the text with the idea that women are oppressed by all men, Wollstonecraft accords all women, including herself, a group identity, a political position from which they can start organizing and agitating.

However, when Wollstonecraft begins to argue at a concrete level, when she confronts, say, the "foibles" of women, that sense of group solidarity dissolves. Notable examples are women's too-ready acceptance of inferior educations, female vanity, and an excessive display of feeling, exemplified in the following passages: First, education—"Led by their dependent situation and domestic employments more into society, what they learn is rather by snatches; and as learning is with them, in general, only a secondary thing, they do not pursue any one branch with that persevering ardour necessary to give vigour to the faculties, and clearness to the judgment" (p. 23). Second, self-involvement—

> It is acknowledged that [females] spend many of the first years of their lives in acquiring a smattering of accomplishments; meanwhile strength of body and mind are sacrificed to libertine no-

tions of beauty, to the desire of establishing themselves,—the only way women can rise in the world,—by marriage. And this desire making mere animals of them, when they marry they act as such children may be expected to act:—they dress; they paint, and nickname God's creatures. Surely these weak beings are only fit for a seraglio!—Can they be expected to govern a family with judgment, or take care of the poor babes whom they bring into the world? (p. 10)

With such attention to vain practices and little intellectual encouragement, women can scarcely be expected to lead (nor do they lead) sensible lives: "Nor can it be expected that a woman will resolutely endeavour to strengthen her constitution and abstain from enervating indulgencies, if artificial notions of beauty, and false descriptions of sensibility, have been early entangled with her motives of action" (p. 43). In censuring how white middle-class women act, Wollstonecraft views them as a homogenized group— "I view, with indignation, the mistaken notions that enslave my sex. . . . It is time to effect a revolution in female manners" (pp. 37, 45). She separates herself from them as a mentor-censor.

Wollstonecraft's self-distancing arises from an understandably positive view she holds of her own ability to transcend situations that she generally deplores in the female population. Since she had broken through prescribed barriers in a rather independent fashion from an early age, she deplores the same lack of resourcefulness in other women; she sees no valid reason why other women cannot act the same way, her sense of female conditioning somewhat precarious. Or perhaps she understands her own social construction and her past inability to remove herself from certain scenarios— when she worked as the irascible Mrs. Dawson's companion, for example. She could be projecting anger at her own passivity in earlier situations.

This sense of herself as set apart comes out even more clearly, though somewhat indirectly, in a footnote to the second *The Rights of Woman*. In the text proper Wollstonecraft is referring to the length of time it will take for slaves—like white women, presumably—to gather themselves up from the condition of slavery: "Man, taking her body, the mind is left to rust; so that while physical love enervates man, as being his favourite recreation, he will endeavour to enslave woman:—and, who can tell, how many generations may be necessary to give vigour to the virtue and talents of the freed posterity of abject slaves" (pp. 76–77).

Wollstonecraft quotes herself in the footnote, stating that slavery always constitutes an untenable human condition: "Supposing that women are voluntary slaves—slavery of any kind is unfavourable to human happiness and improvement" (p. 77). Then she purportedly quotes from an essay by a contemporary, Vicesimus Knox, as follows:

> The subjects of these self-erected tyrants [i.e., those who establish what norm of human affairs will be, either "some rich, gross, unphilosophical man, or some titled frivolous lady, distinguished for boldness, but not for excellence"] are most truly slaves, though voluntary slaves; but as slavery of any kind is unfavourable to human happiness and improvement, I will venture to offer a few suggestions, which may induce the subjugated tribes to revolt, and claim their invaluable birthright, their natural liberty.   (p. 77).

As it turns out Wollstonecraft has altered Knox's quotation to underscore her own political orientation. In his essay Knox was not talking of women, let alone calling them slaves.

Wollstonecraft's fiery response to female domination echoed in Knox's essay—that women should act independently and ignore strictures—is probably why the essay appeals to her so much. Entitled "On the Fear of Appearing Singular," one of the essay's most telling passages encourages such (singular) thought, no matter the consequences or the social ridicule:

> It may not be improper to premise, that to one individual his own natural rights and possessions, of whatever kind, are as valuable as those of another are to that other. It is his own

happiness which is concerned in his choice of principles and conduct. By these he is to stand, or by these to fall.

In making this important choice, then, let the sense of its importance lead him to assert the rights of man. These rights will justify him in acting and thinking, as far as the laws of that community, whose protection he seeks, can allow, according to the suggestions of his own judgment. He will do right to avoid adopting any system of principles, or following any pattern of conduct, which his judgment has not pronounced conducive to his happiness, and consistent with his duties; consistent with those duties which he owes to his God, to his neighbour, to himself, and to his society. Though the small circle with whom he is personally connected may think and act differently, and may even despise and ridicule his singularity, yet let him persevere. His duty, his freedom, his conscience, and his happiness, must appear to every man, who is not hoodwinked, superior to all considerations.[27]

The sense of importance that Wollstonecraft attached to independent or singular thought—a cornerstone of bourgeois individualist ideology—helps to explain her apparent lack of emotional solidarity with the white women she roundly castigates throughout the second *The Rights of Woman*. Although her intentions are unreservedly positive—to restore natural rights to all women—her approach is not entirely compassionate. She sees all around her that women accept cultural standards for themselves. Because she has resisted these norms and short-circuited her own social construction, she deplores women who have not followed suit.

The separation that Wollstonecraft maintains from other women prevents her from seeing the implications of women's response, especially in the common frivolous practices she condemns. She sees, for example, the trope of the coquette as exclusive evidence that women accept their inferiority. The following passage on Rousseau's ideas about women as sexual objects illustrates Wollstonecraft's dislike of teasing behavior. "Rousseau declares that a woman should never, for a moment, feel herself independent, that

19

she should be governed by fear to exercise her natural cunning, and made a coquetish slave in order to render her a more alluring object of desire" (p. 25). Wollstonecraft sees women as slaves to men, not just because of male lust but because women enslave themselves through an obsession with fashion and an eager acceptance of inadequate education. She regards female foibles as evidence of an almost wilful self-trivialization.

Furthermore the blame that Wollstonecraft attaches to white women for their vanity is complicated by her assessment of the relationship between African women and dress:

> The attention to dress, therefore, which has been thought a sexual propensity, I think natural to mankind. But I ought to express myself with more precision. When the mind is not sufficiently opened to take pleasure in reflection, the body will be adorned with sedulous care; and ambition will appear in tattooing or painting it.
>
> So far is this first inclination carried, that even the hellish yoke of slavery cannot stifle the savage desire of admiration which the black heroes inherit from both their parents, for all the hardly earned savings of a slave are expended in a little tawdry finery. And I have seldom known a good male or female servant that was not particularly fond of dress. Their clothes were their riches; and, I argue from analogy, that the fondness for dress, so extravagant in females, arises from the same cause— want of cultivation of mind. [28]

Wollstonecraft equates self-conscious dressing with lack of intellectuality. In doing so she reveals her conditioning as a contemporary woman, bombarded by and receptive to such ideas about Africans as David Hume's: "There never was a civilized nation of any other complexion than white, nor even any individual eminent either in action or speculation. No ingenious manufactures amongst them, no arts, no sciences. . . . Such a uniform and constant difference could not happen, in so many countries and ages, if nature had not made an original distinction betwixt these breeds of men." [29] Wollstonecraft does not address such possibilities as white women's resentment about powerlessness, their displacement of anger, their projection of personal power and pleasure, or, in the case of Africans and African-Caribbeans, she does not take account of customary cultural practices.[30] Given, too, her protestations to Sophie Fuseli about her scrupulous conduct toward the Swiss painter Henry Fuseli (and his toward Mary Wollstonecraft), her attack on coquetry might also betray a rather personal subtext.[31]

Wollstonecraft's views, then, of white women's behavior in particular and of sexual differences in general are complex and self-contradictory.[32] Justifiably she thinks of herself as positively breaking through social constraints while the vast majority of women conforms to a restrictive mandate. She sees this process continuing as a result of practices that reach back to antiquity: "Man, from the remotest antiquity, found it convenient to exert his strength to subjugate his companion, and his invention to shew that she ought to have her neck bent under its yoke; she, as well as the brute creation, was created to do his pleasure" (p. 49).

These contentions parallel ideas expressed in Catharine Macaulay's *Letters on Education,* in which she argues that women are historically oppressed because of situation and circumstances; the only item distinctly separating men and women is physical strength, which men have used to exercise their physical desires freely. The fine differences between them seem to be as follows: Catharine Macaulay wants women to stop being giddy but recognizes their social indoctrination. At one level Wollstonecraft concurs with this and even uses the language of "circumstances" to explain vain and flirtatious female behavior. But she seems much less patient— more desperate, even—with women's situation. Catharine Macaulay is calmer, less rhetorically intense in her analysis, perhaps because with a certain amount of middle-class privilege in her life, the situation has affected her less.

Wollstonecraft's argument from antiquity has further implications. She contends that this age-old subjugation for unspecified reasons enables men's desire to transform women into tools for lust.

These beaten-down women with bent necks resemble the brute creation, *brute* a synonym in contemporary vocabulary for *slaves*. Thus white women, slaves, and oxen become part of a metonymic chain of the tyrannized; this association of colonial slavery with female subjugation opens up new political possibilities, despite its ethnocentric dimension. The bent yoke, for example, suggesting excessive maltreatment also suggests insecurity on the part of the dominant, a combination that precipitates insurrection. The question that permeates the image is who will bear a brutelike status eternally. Remember, too, that the San Domingan revolution is less than a year old, so Wollstonecraft's words inscribe a threat of resistance: "History brings forward a fearful catalogue of the crimes which their cunning has produced, when the weak slaves have had sufficient address to over-reach their masters" (p. 167).

Moreover Wollstonecraft deliberately uses the language of slavery to define women's status: "When, therefore, I call women slaves, I mean in a political and civil sense; for, indirectly they obtain too much power, and are debased by their exertions to obtain "illicit sway" (p. 167). This imposed status, this condition of subjugation, provokes women into the flirtatious behavior she dislikes, but also provokes duplicitous strategies of gaining power. In histories of slave insurrections, the ear of the master—necessary for finding things out and for facilitating the timing of rebellions— was frequently obtained through such illicit sway. While decrying the domestic sabotage of coquetry, she affirms a time-honored slave strategy and the need for resistance. Perhaps most important, Wollstonecraft is suggesting collective opposition, but can only do so through positing the resistance of slaves and the London mob. Put bluntly, Wollstonecraft's conditioning prevents her from suggesting, except very obliquely, that women resist politically—although she herself does.

Wollstonecraft also reemphasizes that the historical subjugation of women is linked to male desire for sexual as well as political and social power. In doing so she fuses the oppression of white women and black female slaves as well as slaves in general. A striking

22

passage from *The Rights of Woman,* based on the trope of sexual abuse, exemplifies the point. It includes one of the few specific references to contemporary African slaves in the second *Vindication,* or in any of Wollstonecraft's texts, for that matter. "Why subject [women] to propriety—blind propriety, if she be capable of acting from a nobler spring, if she be an heir of immortality? Is sugar always to be produced by vital blood? Is one half of the human species, like the poor African slaves, to be subject to prejudices that brutalize them, when principles would be a sure guard, only to sweeten the cup of man?"[33]

The passage announces that slaves and white women are subjected to forceful practices that have no purpose beyond the paltry one of "sweeten[ing] the cup of man." On the one hand slaves should not be expected to give "vital blood" to produce sugar and cater to white British colonial-patriarchal whim and profiteering. On the other hand the "cup of man" symbolically intimates that a female (opponent) is doing the filling of a priest-like man, displaying a chalice of power. This sexual innuendo is consistent with Wollstonecraft's complex sociosexual discourse throughout the *Vindication.* Wollstonecraft's awareness of the generic use of *man* further problematizes her provocative phraseology and the relationship she hints at between sweetening men's cup and "poor African slaves." If only as faint shadows, black female slaves and the specific kind of sexual persecution they endure are ushered into view, interjecting themselves as sexual victims. Aware of political and personal levels, Wollstonecraft subtly denotes sexuality as one of the "prejudices" that brutalize white and black women alike. As Cora Kaplan suggests, "We must remember to read *A Vindication [of the Rights of Woman]* as its author has instructed us, as a discourse addressed mainly to women of the middle class. Most deeply class-bound is its emphasis on sexuality in its ideological expression, as a mental formation, as the source of woman's oppression."[34]

Sex and resistance interact. A coquette's cunning that can overpower (manipulate) men has links to subterfuges and plots by slaves, especially by black female slaves who double as objects of desire. Or Wollstonecraft might recognize, unconsciously at least, that undue attentiveness to one's person means that desire is suppressed and life is lived on almost self-destructive, self-contradictory planes; excess vanity could be double-edged. Wollstonecraft may be mediating the foolishness she ascribes to such vanity. Thus sexuality becomes the site of black female and, by implication, white female resistance. Women use the very object of desire— themselves, their bodies—to thwart those who desire.

In addition and just as important, Wollstonecraft has firm views on cultural difference from at least the late 1780s, most if not all of which are gleaned more from her readings than personal knowledge. I want to outline briefly some of these views culled from reviews between 1787 and the publication of the second *The Rights of Woman*, for these perspectives would have philosophically underpinned analogues in her texts concerning colonial and gender relations.

Wollstonecraft argues, for instance, that external forces cause sexual and racial differences. She had articulated this understanding earlier in a positive review of the Reverend Samuel Stanhope Smith's *An Essay on the Causes of the Variety of Complexion and Figure in the Human Species* (1787). In this review Wollstonecraft writes as if her knowledge of the subject put her in no place to contradict Smith's treatise. Clearly agreeing with his contentions about monogenesis—and denying the conservative argument of innate difference and necessary cultural separations—that God created essentially distinct beings,[35] she offers no additional refutation of polygenesis. Such subjected people as African-Caribbean slaves and white Anglo-Saxon women are prevented from developing and exercising their reason while certain environments have precipitated their alleged propensity for passion. Wollstonecraft agrees with Smith that climate and social conditions are the principal causes of difference among men and women throughout the world: "Different external circumstances, such as the situation of the country, forms of government, religious opinions, etc. have been

24

traced by the ablest politicians as the main causes of distinct national characters" (Stanhope Smith, p. 431).

Above and beyond these differences, she avows, human beings constitute a unity.[36] Moreover Wollstonecraft accepts the received idea that Africans are "untutored savages" with "coarse and deformed features," but concurs with Smith that differential physiognomy arises as an adaptation to climate:

> Agreeable and cultivated scenes compose the features, and render them regular and gay. Wild, and deformed, and solitary forests tend to impress on the countenance an image of their own rudeness. . . . The infinite attentions of polished society give variety and expression to the face. The want of interesting emotions leaving its muscles lax and unexerted, they are suffered to distend themselves to a larger and grosser size, and acquire a soft unvarying swell that is not distinctly marked by any idea.
>
> (Stanhope Smith, pp. 434–35)

Domestic servants, for example, look superior to field slaves. Ultimately, however, education is the cutting edge and creates the "greatest difference between men in society" (p. 437). Whereas she argues in *The Rights of Woman* that attention to dress proves that Africans, conceived in a totalized way, are an unmeditative people, in this reading they become people historically cut off from intellectual pursuit. With a change in circumstances, she argues, reason can replace alleged naïveté and infantilism.[37]

Therefore populations in temperate climates—since they neither look ugly nor think crudely—have benefited. The host of assumptions embedded in these propositions goes unchallenged in the five years from Wollstonecraft's writing of this review to the second *Vindication* and are reinforced in her review in 1789 of Olaudah Equiano's *Interesting Narrative of His Life . . . Written by Himself.* More positive, *The Rights of Woman* subtextually suggests that if everyone switched places, Europeans would be the other. This implication lies dormant, however. Basically, Wollstonecraft contends that such an intellectual endeavor as an autobiography is a curiosity, and more damaging, that Equiano's *Interesting Narrative* "proves" contentions about inferiority: "We shall only observe, that if these volumes do not exhibit extraordinary intellectual powers, sufficient to wipe off the stigma, yet the activity and ingenuity, which conspicuously appear in the character of Gustavus, place him on a par with the general mass of men, who fill the subordinate stations in a more civilized society than that which he was thrown into at his birth" (pp. 27–28). In other words, Equiano is surprisingly on a par with working-class men in Britain. In conclusion Wollstonecraft praises Equiano's descriptions of cultural practice and difference but quietly questions the authenticity of his account. This matches a constant suspicion by the eighteenth-century white middle class about the writings of not only Africans but white working-class women.[38] "Throughout, a kind of contradiction is apparent: many childish stories and puerile remarks, do not agree with some more solid reflections, which occur in the first pages. In the style also we observed a striking contrast: a few well-written periods do not smoothly unite with the general tenor of the language" (pp. 28–29).

Wollstonecraft does, however, make an intervention on the question of sexually abused female slaves. Through reviews and personal reading Wollstonecraft was well attuned to this phenomenon. The review of Equiano's *Interesting Narrative* pinpoints her horror at "the treatment of male and female slaves, on the voyage, and in the West Indies, which make the blood turn its course."[39] In his *Interesting Narrative* Equiano categorically indicts "our clerks and many others at the same time [who] have committed acts of violence on the poor, wretched, and helpless females."[40] In chronicling his feelings on finally leaving Montserrat, Equiano harrows readers by underlining his despondency, disgust, and (silently) his sense of impotence: "I bade adieu to the sound of the cruel whip and all other dreadful instruments of torture; adieu to the offensive sight of the violated chastity of the sable females, which has too often accosted my eyes."[41]

In addition to her acquaintance with Equiano's firsthand experiences, Wollstonecraft has presented a paradigm of slavery in an extract on Inkle and Yarico in *The Female Reader*. Shipwrecked British merchant Inkle is rescued and nursed back to health by islander Yarico. After they fall in love, Inkle promises to take Yarico to London and treat her royally, but when a rescue ship appears, Inkle cavalierly sells her to slave traders when their ship docks in Barbados. To top off his inhumanity, after Yarico pleads for mercy on account of her pregnancy, Inkle "only made use of that information to rise in his demands upon the purchaser."[42]

Hence Wollstonecraft subtly contests the sexual abuse of black women in the vital blood passage, in reviewing Equiano and in spotlighting that last look at a pregnant Yarico in an anthology for adolescent girls. Since her discourse as a white woman is already shockingly untraditional, to speak of sex, and of all things to speak openly of black women's sexuality and hint at abuse suffered at the hands of white planters, would be an untenable flouting of social propriety. She has to maintain a semblance of conventional gender expectations.

On the site of the body and sex, then, Wollstonecraft foregrounds the relationship between black and white women and their common point of rebellion. At one point when she refers to women as "brown and fair" (meaning dark and fair-haired white women), the slippage and connection between black and white women reopens a fissure of sorts for comparing overlapping oppressions. For example, slave auctions and the marriage market are represented as variations on activities that are not life-enhancing to African-Caribbean and Anglo-Saxon women.[43] Nonetheless Wollstonecraft acknowledges by her loaded silences that the representation of others' sexuality as well as sexual self-representation is a tricky business.[44] Thus in one sense equal rights and a self-denying sexuality go hand in hand because sexuality for Wollstonecraft (dictated at large by men) imperils any chances of female autonomy. Not only that, Wollstonecraft recognizes dissimilar codings for white female and bondswomen's bodies, differences in complicity and coercion. In keeping with her sense of singularity and in part because she is closer to them, she is much harder on middle-class white women. She does not feel affected by or implicated in female social conditioning. Unlike Catharine Macaulay, who argues that women will "come to" only if they understand their oppression, Wollstonecraft implicitly recommends imitation of her own bold behavior as the wake-up call. To recap briefly: All women have the same choices as she did and should forgo vanity and self-indulgence; they should break their "silken fetters." If she can short-circuit subjugation, her brief goes, anyone can.

Thus beyond a rhetorical appeal to effect a revolution in female manners, Wollstonecraft tends to eschew a group response to the absence of female rights. Furthermore this aloofness permeates—even undercuts—her sense of vindication. Instead, a buried sense of identification and solidarity expresses itself in a displaced way.

Specifically Wollstonecraft talks about resistance only by talking about slaves. The successful revolution by slaves in San Domingo taught the British public that slaves and freed blacks could collectively overthrow systematic tyranny. By equating slaves with laboring-class "mobs" and using highly inflated diction for rebels, Wollstonecraft censures slaves' reaction. "For the same reason," states Wollstonecraft, quoting from Jean-Jacques Rousseau, "women have, or ought to have, but little liberty; they are apt to indulge themselves excessively in what is allowed them. Addicted in every thing to extremes, they are even more transported at their diversions than boys." She continues this response to Rousseau: "The answer to this is very simple. Slaves and mobs have always indulged themselves in the same excesses, when once they broke loose from authority.—The bent bow recoils with violence, when the hand is suddenly relaxed that forcibly held it."[45]

Yet, since Wollstonecraft disdains passivity and servitude, she may be embedding an unconscious desire about female resistance that corresponds to her own. She could be hinting that women should emulate the San Domingo insurgents and fight back. That nuance is stressed pictorially by the sexual overtones of female compliance in "bent bow." Just as important, the image resonates with the previous textual image of women from earliest times with necks bent under a yoke.

Put succinctly, what slaves can do, white women can do; as she asserts in *The Rights of Woman*, authority and the reaction to it push the "crowd of subalterns forward."[46] Sooner or later tyranny incites retaliation. San Domingo instructs women in the importance of connecting physical and moral agency. Struggle creates a potential bridge from ignorance to consciousness and self-determination. In the most hard-hitting sense, the San Domingo revolutionaries loudly voice by their bold example—to anyone ready to listen—that challenge to oppression is not an option but a responsibility. The social and political status quo is anything but fixed.

Wollstonecraft's metaphor of the bent bow also reminds readers that male tyrants and predators provoke their own crossfire; at some point those who are bowed may uncoil themselves and assault the bender.

This image of the bent bow further recalls Wollstonecraft's own situation in the previous decade. Undeterred by an unnerving home life, she tried her hand at most of the humdrum occupations open to women, refusing to be molded or deterred by social prescription. Befriending and being befriended by Dissenters like Richard Price only fortified Wollstonecraft's already firm opposition to women's lot. Moreover her subtle, analogous, and multiply voiced threats address at least two major audiences. She overtly advises women to educate themselves and warns men that vengeance can strike from several directions. The fierce, conservative reaction to *The Rights of Woman* is a response to the covert as well as the overt text.

In that sense the wheel comes almost full circle. Wollstonecraft recognizes that all women are opposed by all men in a general group identity. However, because she privileges personal and political singularity and takes pride in independent thought and action, she identifies her own resistance to gendered tyranny as the means by which women should subvert domination. She projects outward from her personal response to female exploitation, oblivious to more devious practices on the part of other females to assert themselves and gain at least some personal, if not political, power. In one sense her bourgeois individualism prevents that insight because she sees herself as outside customary female assimilation. Faced with oppression women have simply made wrong choices. Consequently Wollstonecraft can posit collective rebellion by white women to prescribed subordination only by analogy.

With this displaced reaction in mind, Wollstonecraft's diatribe against female reactions to males—their flirtatious behavior—can be read more sympathetically. Just as Wollstonecraft can indict Africans for being neither intellectual nor reflexive while portraying a carefully executed and successful revolution, so, too, does she exhibit a conflicted stance toward women. Since slaves resist masters and since all men oppress all women, women will, by implication, resist their male masters. Thus Wollstonecraft registers indirectly that women could resist through coquettish manipulation, however feeble or distorted.[47]

This argument about "slaves and mobs" creates a fissure in the text. If one doubles back to, say, salient passages where Wollstonecraft condemns Rousseau—Woman "should be governed by fear," he says, "to exercise her natural cunning, and made a coquetish slave" (p. 25)—Wollstonecraft's view of the resistances of "slaves and mobs" becomes open to reinterpretation: Even though she assaults these self-trivializing behaviors and deplores their forms, at some level she may recognize them as tropes of insurrection; she uses female reaction to male domination in a plural way. Deploring how women try to finesse and please men through sexual maneuvering, she rhetorically conflates *coquettish* with *cunning* and makes sexual manipulation double as a form of resistance to oppression. Women play at blind obedience not only to get some of what they want but unconsciously to ridicule their "masters," to cancel out tyranny with emotional excess, with a mirror-image perversion of power. Frivolous giggling is also a signal act of mimicry whereby women seem to conform to expectations. Ironically the artificiality of forced laughing marks male desire and orthodox prescriptions for female behavior.

Mary Wollstonecraft and Slavery

If Wollstonecraft is (unconsciously or not) subtly mocking the idea that fear works as a governing principle to produce obedience, she foregrounds the idea that forced obedience linked to sex is a practice that can turn into its opposite: Women will mimic the master's desire with design, they will use conformist ideas about womanhood to gain power. At times Wollstonecraft recognizes these strategies more openly. Thus Wollstonecraft inscribes and heralds a central thematic in texts about women's relation to colonialism and postcolonialism: the special role and burden of women's sexual subordination. The state of warfare that subsists between the sexes (races) makes them (the tyrannized group) employ those ruses or "illicit sway" that often frustrate more open strategies of force.

The aim of *The Rights of Woman*, then, is to vindicate women's rights. Foregrounding how female sexuality is linked to degrading patriarchal practice and self-demeaning personal and public behavior is integral—however subtly—to that *Vindication*. Starting from the premise that all women are oppressed by all men, Wollstonecraft subscribes to a concept of overall group identity. This is undercut, however, when she probes particulars because her sense of a personally wrought self-determination causes her to find women culpable for their vanity, their acceptance of an inferior education, their emphasis on feeling. She locates herself outside what she deems self-demeaning behavior.

In the end she posits a group response indirectly, only by looking at oppressed communities who have actively resisted—slaves in particular—and sometimes "mobs." Her suppressed sense of solidarity and her identification with women are expressed through the rebellion of slaves whose bow (back) has been bent too far. This analogy also constitutes a threat to masters; contradiction is there from the beginning since all men are oppositional—within Wollstonecraft's political framework—to all women.

Put another way, Mary Wollstonecraft's construction within specific social and cultural boundaries, which she resists, produces a covert text. Her sense of personal singularity occludes her vision so she cannot always imagine or conceptualize flirtation as a tool of resistance. Despite a radical outlook, moreover, she still subscribes to a sense of class hierarchy that contradicts her demands for greater distribution of wealth and legal representation and for female independence and colonial emancipation. In that sense her text brilliantly illuminates the bourgeois project of liberation. She embodies the liberal ideal of progress in demanding freedom in certain individuals, but the shortcomings inherent in that ideal undercut it. The conditions that produced the text, then, end up questioning the text itself and highlighting its gaps and incompletions, its long series of tensions between bourgeois values and issues of class, race, gender, and desire. So deeply estranged from its internal conflicts is *The Rights of Woman* that it cannot ideologically fulfill itself; an authentic, workable solution to female subjugation is impossible. Wollstonecraft's liberal, individualist perspective will not let her see that what is common to both white/black and male/female power relations is the concept of private property itself: Europeans see Africans as chattel; men own "their women." Thus, she collapses an effect into a cause. The text trips over itself, its variant vindications ideologically incompatible. As a result contradiction emerges as a major textual coherence, problem solving beyond reach.

Additionally, because the text invokes the French and San Domingo revolutions, the complexity of sexual difference, inequities perpetrated against Dissenters, and the Abolition Movement, textual implosions inevitably occur. Even while the text appears to dampen inflammatory ideas and underwrite the current system, liberating ideas erupt to refute the self-contradictory discourse of bourgeois feminism.

Thus the issues that Wollstonecraft avoids or bypasses end up hollowing and shaping the text into a new determination. She talks about disaffection, yet often blames women's alienation on their own behavior; she poses the problem as one for which women bear responsibility. Her sociocultural myopia leads her to misread resistance. Concurrently she undermines her own argument through parallels between white women and black slaves. Moreover the condition of women that she illuminates pinpoints an important area of sexual differences and pushes the frontiers of this debate forward. Put baldly, the text ironically subverts the very bourgeois ideology it asserts (which creates alienation) and demands rights for white middle-class women despite the restrictive system it promotes.

Furthermore Wollstonecraft's usage of colonial slavery as a reference point for female subjugation launches a new element into the discourse on women's rights. It is no coincidence, then, that Charlotte Smith in *Desmond* (1792) and Mary Hays in *Memoirs of Emma Courtney* (1796) criticize colonial slavery along with discussions of women's rights; following Mary Wollstonecraft, they use slavery as the premier sign of the antithesis of individual freedom. They explore popular controversies, simultaneously alluding to Wollstonecraft's innovative investigations and connections. First, their inscription of colonial slavery presupposes the presence of women of color and assumes a white, evolving, patriarchal class system as its common enemy. Second, it suggests unity among the colonized and their allies. Third, it centerstages the question of sexuality in gender relations and stresses the ubiquity of sexual abuse in qualitatively different environments.

By theorizing about women's rights using old attributions of harem-based slavery in conjunction with denotations of colonial slavery, Wollstonecraft was a political pioneer, fundamentally altering the definition of rights and paving the way for a much wider cultural dialogue.

The Hart Sisters: Early
African-Caribbean
Educators and
the "Thirst for Knowledge"

[The San Domingo revolution], that first and
indelible image of reversed power, black power,
which rocked France for decades.
—Christopher Miller, *Blank Darkness*, p. 109

Introduction: Family Background and Methodism

Six years after Mary Wollstonecraft wrote the second *The Rights of Woman*, two similarly tough-minded and independent sisters in Antigua, Anne Hart Gilbert (1773–1833) and Elizabeth Hart Thwaites (1772–1833), tackled related issues. Like Mary Wollstonecraft they were educators and proponents of human rights but, more important, critical differences separated them from Mary Wollstonecraft. The Hart sisters lived, for example, in a colonized-country; they were African-Caribbean women; they argued that social conditions alone produced what appeared to be racial difference; they actively tried to improve the status of slaves; and in pre-abolition days they supported emancipation. Little known, these sisters produced an abundance of historically significant texts that included political manifestos, polemics on slavery, poems, hymns, and controversial letters.

The Hart sisters' grandmother was Frances Clearkley, an African-Caribbean convert to Methodism under the ministry of Francis Gilbert, Nathaniel Gilbert's brother. Their paternal grandfather was Timothy Clearkley. "My grandmother," states Anne Hart Gilbert, "reserv'd her first [admission] Ticket [to a Methodist meeting] pinned in the rules of the Society."[1] Frances Clearkley must have been a free woman of color; otherwise her daughter would have been a slave because in slave society the mother's status determined the children's. The original membership of the Hart family within the community known officially as the free colored community probably derived from this marriage.

Their mother was Frances Clearkley's pious daughter Anne, who married Barry Conyers Hart, an African-Caribbean plantation owner.[2] A troubleshooter and poet who wrote for the local newspaper, he owned an estate in Popeshead, near St. John's. Known as a man who agonized over punishments and tried to act humanely toward his slaves, Barry Conyers Hart clearly took his conflictual role as a planter to heart. Hart's convictions matched those of Methodism's founder, emancipationist John Wesley, who influenced his attitudes—most black slaveowners were notoriously hard taskmasters.[3] On one occasion Hart spent a weekend in the homes of task-gang members to acquire a better sense of slaves' way of life. Before traveling missionaries ministered on a regular basis, his home functioned as a site of public worship. Hart helped slaves execute their affairs by preparing their manumission papers and offering general advice, which was unconventional for these virulently proslavery times and especially for a member of the plantocratic class. This he undertook without charging.

Hart's role as a black slaveholder signified the complex position occupied by the free colored communities in Antiguan society. Like the slaves they abhorred subordination, and like slaves they were buried with criminals and suicides in a separate cemetery: "Even the bell used to toll the death of a colored person was inferior in size and quality to that which announced the death of a white colonist."[4] Yet they also resembled the entrenched white ruling class in owning slaves. Politically, that is, they occupied a critical intersecting zone between both groups. Their value to the ruling class meant that to a limited extent, their legal demands were noted and sometimes accommodated.

Most prominent among the sisters' texts were the histories of Methodism written by each sister in 1804 in response to a request to do so by the Reverend Richard Pattison. Pattison, a new Methodist missionary on Nevis sent out from England, probably wanted information for the Society's records from members of the free colored community about the African-Caribbean version of the island's Methodist history.[5] Anne Hart Gilbert also wrote a related biography of her pious husband, John Gilbert. The Antiguan Methodist church to which the sisters' family belonged was dominated in its early days by several households—the Clearkleys, the Cables, the Lynches, and the Gilberts—that fostered a sense of independence. The Gilberts were related to Nathaniel Gilbert, who introduced Methodism to the West Indies.[6] The Hart sisters were connected to all four families. By the time the sisters converted, Methodism had become a culturally dominant institution in Antigua: "By the end of 1786, when Dr. Coke made his dramatic entrance into the religious history of the West Indies, Baxter had made about two thousand converts in Antigua, and the Negroes had built a house in St. John's Town, where meetings were held."[7] The Methodist missions also began to concentrate on the conversion of slaves.

Furthermore, as members of distinguished Methodist families and privy to female-administered religious instruction, Anne and Elizabeth Hart were dedicated to conversion, especially of laboring and enslaved people. In the words of a contemporary Methodist historian, the Reverend John Horsford:

> In most cases, however, a mother, or sometimes a grandmother, and that maternal ancestor perfectly black, or nearly so, was a devotee of Methodism, sang its hymns with rapture, loved its Class-Meetings, delighted in its Lovefeasts, heard its tenets from the lips of its Ministers with avidity. . . . These females have each led with them to the Wesleyan chapel a little boy or girl, initiating them into the habit of attending the church of the coloured people, since the "big church"—so called—was, in those days, intended for greater folk; and, more than this, they conducted such boys and girls to the Sunday-school.[8]

The evangelical household of the Hart-Clearkley-Cable family pursued such charitable activities as visiting the sick and distributing Bibles. The Hart sisters also grew up in a cultural atmosphere in which the writings of John Milton and William Cowper—celebrated nonconformists—were admired. Many of their philanthropic activities were anathema to the Antiguan ruling class, since the governor, the council, the magistracy, and numerous Assembly House members all subscribed to the Anglican church.[9]

During the first year of the ministry of Thomas Coke, a renowned Methodist missionary who arrived in Antigua in 1786, Anne and Elizabeth Hart were received into the Methodist church and baptized. Following John Wesley's example, Coke did not mention emancipation as a specific principle.[10] After their conversion the sisters changed their habits, dressed plainly, and renounced what they considered to be worldly pursuits. Elizabeth Hart stopped playing the piano because music, she felt, "drew her heart from better things."[11]

Anne Hart Gilbert

Anne Hart Gilbert's *History of Methodism* discusses her conversion and in that sense doubles as a spiritual autobiography. Thus she subscribed to John Wesley's belief in rigorous self-examination as part of recording and maintaining the conversion experience.[12] She proudly relates her own personal transition from "vilest reptile me" (p. 10) to the ecstasy of conversion. Although she ostensibly fashions an image of herself as humble and vulnerable, she still locates herself among the spiritually committed who record conversion. Without vanity she nurtures an appropriate sense of personal power and exemplary status. In her own words:

> It will swell this Letter to size almost enormous, to tell you all the love and watchful care that has covered my defenceless head; or to particularize those events that have united together all the links in the chain of Providence, which has been working together for my good ever since I came into existence but unnoted by me, 'till the scales of pride; ignorance & unbelief, fell from my eyes, by the light & power which accompanies the Gospel faithfully preached. Let it suffice that I add my feeble testimony to that of innumerable multitudes, that "God is no respecter of persons"—That "He willeth not the death of a Sinner"—That he hath never failed the feeblest nor the most unworthy that ever confided in his promises. He hath been with me, according to his faithful word, "Thro the Water & the Fire." He has upheld me (tho' in seasons of sore trial & temptation, The floods have lifted up their voice, & the waves seem'd ready to o'er whelm my frighted soul, yet, "The Lord has been mightier than the noise of many waters, Yea than the mighty waves of the Sea." I can indeed adopt the "language of the Psalmist & say—"O how great is thy goodness which thou "hast laid up for them that fear thee, which thou has wrought for them that trust in thee before the Sons of men, Thou didst hide me in thy secret presense from the pride of man: Thou didst keep me secretly in a pavilion from the strife of tongues." Blessed be his name, He is indeed my strength & my Son, & is become my Salvation; And by his power I will rest upon his faithfulness while I sojourn in this vale of tears, 'till my last change shall come, & then I trust thro' grace to join the innumerable multitude in ascribing, Blessing,

& glory, & wisdom & thanksgiving and honor & power & might unto our God forever and ever. Amen.[13]

Anne Hart's conversion closely followed the death of her mother in 1785, after which she assumed a surrogate maternal role toward her siblings until she married in 1798. While instructing her siblings for thirteen years, Anne Hart, aided by her sister Elizabeth, also offered religious instruction to slaves and taught them to read. This was a remarkable decision for any woman to make during the late slave period, when the institution of slavery was under attack and the character of society was gradually changing.[14] Such activities discomfited the Antiguan population, which feared the spread of nonconforming religious practices and ideas.[15] Successful conversions flouted the entrenched colonial order and smacked of potential unrest. The colonial bureaucracy feared that ideas of spiritual equality generated a vocabulary about rights that jeopardized white safety. During this period, moreover, slaves and free colored people waged a triumphant revolution in San Domingo that threatened the overall stability of the Caribbean.

In Britain meanwhile, the antislavery movement had successfully pressed for a parliamentary vote in 1793. The discourse of abolition and emancipation had not only broken loose but was moving transatlantically. The controversial activities that marked both sisters as abolitionists were matched by the marriages of Anne and Elizabeth Hart to two white men, John Gilbert and Charles Thwaites, respectively. The backlash from Anne Hart's wedding indicates how high feeling ran in a racially tense society.

Despite white ruling-class opposition and internal prejudice from Methodists themselves, Anne Hart Gilbert married John Gilbert, cousin of Nathaniel Gilbert, in 1798. John Gilbert had joined the Methodists in 1794 and become a class leader and preacher by 1797.[16] His first wife died soon afterward. As a white lay preacher he was already in trouble for his views on black-white relations. Fellow officers in the militia criticized him for referring to slaves in his congregation as "brothers"; any such familiarity, they felt, imperiled white control in a plantocratic society. They threatened court-martial, which Gilbert pointedly ridiculed, and he was never summoned (Box, p. 21).

After he proposed, both Anne Hart and her father tried to dissuade Gilbert from such a socially proscribed alliance. Perhaps they feared some physical violence. They suggested that he travel to England, but since Gilbert, in his own words, "had not the means of paying the expense of travelling . . . I therefore persisted" (Box, p. 23). One week later Anne Hart accepted his offer.

In the governor's absence the president of the council as well as the superintendent of the Wesleyan mission, John Baxter, advised him against marriage to Anne Hart. Such was the rarity of miscegenous alliances that Baxter warned Gilbert he would be "committed to jail as a madman."[17] The same fellow officers again disavowed Gilbert and attempted to court-martial him, whereupon he resigned his commission (Box, p. 24). As a further mark of public censure he was deprived of his commission as a notary public. Someone threw into the sea the painted sign advertising his business outside the business office. After he was refused a marriage license, he published the banns in church, despite the fact that one of his relatives asked all Antiguan clergymen not to marry them. A wry John Gilbert comments on these activities in his autobiography:

> I was informed that he [this relative] also wrote to the naval Commander-in-Chief, requesting him to forbid all the Chaplains of His Majesty's ships on the station to perform the office.
>
> It is proper to observe, that if I had determined upon seducing and degrading the object of my regard and esteem, I should have been considered by the ungodly aristocracy of the country as having acted quite properly, and incurred no reproach from them, as she was a woman of colour. (Box, p. 25)

In *Antigua and the Antiguans* the expansive Antiguan commentator Frances Lanaghan puts it this way: "Slaves and free black females were often expected to become the mistresses of white men," or, in West Indian terminology, *housekeeper.* [18]

Having provoked public outrage, John Gilbert and Anne Hart Gilbert returned from their honeymoon to find the door of his office painted a symbolic half white, half yellow. Who married them remains a mystery. In 1803 the couple moved from St. Johns to English Harbour, a neighboring town a few miles south, where John Gilbert was promoted as first clerk to the storekeeper in the royal naval yard.

Anne Hart Gilbert's earlier attack on the suppression of religious instruction and information to slaves is paralleled by her renewed assault on white immorality. Once again the attack intertextualizes not simply the discourse of abolition but subverts and reverses customary mythologies about black immorality. When she and her husband arrive in English Harbour in 1803, for example, she explains how immoral whites masquerading as missionaries have scandalized "a small society of black & colour people, consisting of 28 Members & all but a very few in earnest for Salvation. They have never had one half the advantages of the people of St. Johns, having no place of worship to go to on Sundays, & very few of them able to read the word of God." [19] At one blow she censures white apostates, applauds the judgment of the community, radiates moral command, and distances herself and her constituency from cultural practices like obeah and corrupt white spiritual authority. She indicts past white leaders with impunity. [20] Evangelicals loathed any signs of worldliness, idleness, or immorality among those in authority. Respectability mattered.

Anne Hart Gilbert simultaneously criticizes missionary wives. In doing so she dismantles old paradigms about black women (unlike white women, especially missionary wives) as preeminently sexual beings:

> I have at times been grieved to see some of the Wives of our preachers that have been like works for [Flatterers] and [Syco-phants] to shoot at; Who deceived, by what is falsely called,

41

(and bears a strong resemblance to) Kindness & hospitality; & under the idea of doing good, & winning souls to Christ by familiarity with the World, have lost their simplicity, & dead-ness, to the world, been shorn of their spiritual strength & had their affections estranged from the real people of God.[21]

Methodism will be better purified, she strongly suggests, by its black practitioners; conversion will render slaves upstanding citizens. Im-plied in her argument, too, is the contention that social environ-ment alone separates blacks from whites:

The great civilization of the Slaves, their gradual emergence, from the depths of ignorance and barbarism, has imperceptibly had an over-awing effect upon the System of tyranny & cruel oppression that was formerly exercised over them with little or no restraint when they differed in so few respects from the Beasts that perish; And as a natural consequence, those that are set over them feel more cautious in dealing with rational creatures than they did with beings imbruted in ev'ry way both body & mind. The Slaves in general that attend a Gospel ministry, whether they are subject themselves to Church discipline or not, become more creditable & decent in their families and manners than those that do not.   (Gilbert, pp. 20–21)

Anne Gilbert then goes on to underscore subtle but ubiquitous endorsement of black equality by stressing slaves' intellectual hun-ger that would dissolve existing arguments on behalf of innate racial differences. In her own words: "There is in all a thirst for a knowl-edge. The greater part of those that can afford it get themselves taught to read & some to write also. There are hundreds of black & colour children sent to school every year in this little Island; and the great change wrought in the manners & condition of all people of this description is beyond any thing that could have been expected and such as nothing could effect but the wisdom & power of God."[22]

Even more boldly, later in her *History of Methodism* Anne Hart Gilbert indirectly affirms the methods of the San Domingan revolutionaries. She is thankful that Antigua can achieve emancipation peacefully: "Its having been effected by the Un-bloody Sword of truth that has almost unperceivedly cut its way thro' mountainous obstacles; And not by tumultuous distracting revolution, massacre & bloodshed, is cause of unspeakable thankfulness to God" (Gilbert, p. 21).

As if to underscore her pride in the contributions tendered by African-Caribbean people to Antiguan history, Anne Hart Gilbert makes a point of documenting the role played by two black Methodist women at the time she was born. It was a well-known fact of Methodist Antiguan history that when John Baxter arrived on the island in 1778, only African-Caribbeans remained in the Society. Specifically she foregrounds the two women's actions in maintaining a Methodist presence in Antigua, a "praying remnant," after Nathaniel and Francis Gilbert left. In the *History of Methodism* she extols the women as follows:

> Tho' it cannot be said, that they abounded in knowledge, brightness of reason or soundness of speech, yet I say would to God there was the same simplicity, purity & love of the cross in only one half of our greatly increased Society now. The leaders of them were Mary Alley a Mulatto Woman & Sophia Campbel a black. The former after wading thro many trials & temptations is still alive & steady in the good cause. The latter went to her eternal rest in the year 1799. They met together for reading, singing & prayers & with many prayers watered the seed sown by their fathers in the Gospel.[23]

She goes on to state that Mary Alley and Sophia Campbel "ventured in faith to agree for a spot of land to build a chapel upon," although other church members discouraged their project:

> The most decent, and creditable of the black women did not think it a labour too servile to carry stones and marl, to help with their own hands to clear the Land of the rubbish that lay about it, & to bring ready-dressed victuals for the men that were employed in building the House of God. They now rejoiced to

sell their Earrings & bracelets and to buy Lumber & pay Carpenters, to forward this blessed work; and at last they got a comfortable little Chapel, which soon became too small.[24]

Anne Hart Gilbert firmly insists on women's right to pursue God's work and stake out moral ground. She presses the viewpoints in public of individuals customarily refused representability. Having spoken of black women's important historical role in the late eighteenth century, she turns her attention to the present day. In succession she comments on her own relationship with the black community and reaffirms the complex roles black women are forced to play. The slave community, she avows, treats her observations differently from those of the white missionaries. She uses her comments on these observations to declare her unity with that community and her counterhegemonic views regarding the community's received status:

> My complexion exempted me from those prejudices & that disgust which the instability of their white Brethren had planted in their hearts & they tremblingly ventured to receive us as friends. Mr Baxter desired the women to meet with me; I soon found that they were all desirous to have a little Chapel, & to have service on Sundays; & at the time Mr [Matthew] Lumb laboured here had collected five *joes* among themselves for that purpose but it was never brought into effect. I told them how our Sisters in St Johns had heartily united together and even labor'd with their hands to forward the building of the Chapel, & they generally agree to do the same. Previous to our coming here they had been in treaty for a house for the purpose of preaching, but the situation is so hot, and so low, that both Preacher, & hearers, run the risk of getting sick as soon as they come into the open air. We have therefore petitioned the Commissioner to give us a Grant of Land to build in a more convenient place & he has readily granted the petition.[25]

As a black Antiguan herself, Anne Hart Gilbert demands equal religious treatment with whites and implicitly clears a space for a general argument about social and political equality. She refuses to grant any credence to received ideas of innate inferiority, of Africans as brutes. She insists on the recognition of human equality. Lurking in her text is the notion that human exclusion is as sinful as missionary wives' immorality. Secular and spiritual transgression slide into each other.

She further argues that environment and financial exigency create a series of problems that preponderantly affect and objectify women in a racially segregated society. More specifically, she is able to use her philanthropic activities to recode assumptions about the sexuality of female slaves. For example, in response to the number of orphans and children of "fallen and depraved relatives," she and her sister organize a Female Refuge Society.[26] As a result of petitioning, evangelical British women sent money and clothes to support this activity.[27]

Furthermore, Anne Hart Gilbert graphically condemns prostitution along the same lines; culture and economics, not "natural pagan behavior," have produced the social phenomenon. Here she indirectly refutes common contentions about "natural" black female depravity and sexual excess: "I see with heart-felt joy that prostitution is now esteemed abominable & disgraceful by the greater part of the Colour'd Women in St Johns where the great bulk of them reside; and lawful alliances take place as frequently among them as among the whites. This is one happy effect of seeing themselves, examples corroborating, those truths that recommend, chastity tho' accompanied with labour & self-denial" (Gilbert, p. 20).

In many of her social and spiritual activities, Anne Hart Gilbert worked hand in hand with her sister Elizabeth. Before assessing Anne Hart Gilbert's role as an abolitionist and an educator, I turn to her sister Elizabeth's contribution to Antiguan cultural life.

Elizabeth Hart Thwaites

A year younger than her sister Anne, Elizabeth Hart carved out a special political niche as an educator, an antislavery polemicist, and a political activist. According to her own testimony, she had been committed to abolition from a very young age: "I was no sooner capable of thinking, than my heart shuddered at the cruelties that were presented to my sight; but more have I felt since I began to think seriously. I am, however, most concerned to have the evils within rectified, or rather cured; this will perhaps render some of those that are without less poignant, though I do not expect that religion will deliver me from fellow-feeling, nor do I desire it should."[28]

Grace Clearkley Cable, their mother's sister, had introduced Elizabeth Hart to Moravianism as a young girl and influenced her religious conversion. Commitment to the Moravians may account for her ardent early espousal of abolitionist principles.

Bear in mind, too, that in 1793 in Antigua there were 36 whites in the Methodist Society and 1,522 blacks and "people of mixed blood" (Goveia, p. 294). Beyond being continually involved with members of the black communities, both free and enslaved, Elizabeth Hart speaks of her distress at the condition slaves endured. As a member of a prominent family in a community of free people of color, moreover, she undoubtedly knew that the number of community members was increasing while the number of whites was declining. And even though "their whole number [the free colored] at Antigua amounts to only a few Hundred," that community occupied an important political position as a buffer between the ruling class and the slaves (Goveia, p. 96).

More specifically, Elizabeth Hart wrote a letter from her father's estate at Popeshead to a male friend in October 1794—two years after the publication of A *Vindication of the Rights of Woman*—in which she argues from the standpoint of a highly self-conscious emancipationist: "[What matters is] the noble attempt should be made for the abolition of the African Slave-Trade. For what event can human wisdom foresee, more likely to 'give His Son the heathen for His inheritance, and the uttermost parts of the earth for His possession,' than the success of such an enterprise? What will restore the lustre of the Christian name, too long sullied with oppression, cruelty, and injustice" (Hart, "Letter," p. 17). She had, she confided, previously disclosed these views to no one but her sister: "I find some disposed to receive such hard sayings; and why? Because they are not disinterested, self is concerned; and as I cannot, to please the best and wisest, lower the standard of right, or bend a straight rule to favour a crooked practice, I am, for the most part, silent" (Hart, "Letter," p. 1).

However, Elizabeth Hart also knows the difficulty of espousing abolitionist views in Antigua in 1794. Especially between 1787 and 1793 the cause of abolition, let alone emancipation, was deeply unpopular in the colonies where legislators had continually tangled with a British government involved in a serious debate over abolition.

Just as much to the point, Elizabeth Hart's letter appeared when the British parliamentary debate over slavery had temporarily ground to a standstill because of the French Revolution in 1789 and the consequent fear of Jacobinism in England. Even more germane to the colonies, the debate halted because of the successful San Domingo Revolution in 1791; it shocked island colonists to learn that a neighboring island was on an unprecedented route to independence. In response to these events the white colonial class regarded slaves and the population of free people of color even more suspiciously. As slaves slipped out of still colonized islands and sailed to freedom, rumors abounded.[29]

The necessity for emancipation notwithstanding, Elizabeth Hart foregrounds religion as the fundamental priority in human life. Like her sister she emphasizes piety and moral propriety. San Domingo insurrectionists without religion are not "one whit better than ever they were" (Hart, "Letter," p. 16). However, Elizabeth Hart does mediate her commitment to religion somewhat by her implied support for the revolutionary struggle in San Domingo. Her religious principles contest her support for just agitation; she is conflicted about her primary desire. For example, she states that she had heard "strange accounts" about the revolution, "many of them [the slaves] having taken their master's places." She goes on to state that "the oppressors are now the oppressed," rather than the reverse, wording that indicates a positive stand on the revolution. Her exultant final statement over whites being unable to touch the black rebels corroborates her nuanced underwriting of the revolution: "I believe, with a good man, that 'present impunity is the deepest revenge' " (Hart, "Letter," p. 17). Perhaps with the triumph of San Domingo in mind, Elizabeth Hart scoffs at her corresponding advice to "guard our minds against unnecessary solicitude at evils which we cannot remedy" (Hart, "Letter," p. 9).

Instead she fulminates against atrocities she witnessed, tendering toward slaves the very solicitude he recommends against: "[There is a] black train of ills which I know to be inseparably connected with *this* species of slavery: such as may you never know, if it will give you needless pain,—such as my eyes see, and my ears hear daily, and makes my heart shrink when I write" (Hart, "Letter," p. 10).

Hart then assails family fracture, a favored thematic in antislavery discourse. However, one crucial difference separates Elizabeth Hart's diatribe from the polemic of British women writers: Elizabeth Hart is bringing firsthand experience to bear. Consequently her prose avoids the formulaic conventions of late eighteenth-century poems about slavery; it is studded instead with commentary on things she observed. Thus Elizabeth Hart underwrites the importance of the issue, however formulaically it is presented, but intensifies the debate with authentic detail:

It appears to me that pains are taken to prevent, or break, the nearest alliances, often in times of sickness and distress, and sometimes from the basest views. On the neighboring estates the sick are removed from their comfortable abodes to large, hot rooms, made for the purpose, where frequently husbands and wives, parents and children, have no intercourse but through the grates. This is to prevent their lying by longer than necessity obliges; many make their escape from these dark abodes to those blessed regions "where tyrants vex not, and the weary rest." I know several who have been mothers of ten children, who never had the satisfaction to call *one* their own; and this, not from the hand of death, or separation by mutual consent; but sold, given away, or otherwise disposed of, according to the will of man. (Hart, "Letter," p. 11)

At the same time she indirectly wards off unilateral contentions about black inferiority that could apply to her own family and community. She suggests that all black families, enslaved or free, could live in harmony as the Clearkley and Hart families do. All African-Caribbeans lack is opportunity.

Between her espousal of abolitionist views and her *History of Methodism*, Elizabeth Hart married Charles Thwaites, a white Antiguan educator. In 1805, following her marriage in St. Johns where Thwaites was an instructor, the couple moved to English Harbour to join the Gilberts. Within a decade she and her sister had become important Methodist educators and part of the Society's ruling class circle. It is not surprising that Elizabeth Hart Thwaites also was invited by the Reverend Richard Pattison to write a *History of Methodism* ten years after her abolitionist letter to a friend in 1794. More public than her letter and oriented in a more overtly spiritual direction, the *History of Methodism* reiterates her abolitionist views and foregrounds in a dramatically different way her position as a female representative of the black (Methodist) population. Once again the *History of Methodism* doubles as a conversion narrative or spiritual autobiography.

However, Elizabeth Hart focuses on her positive relations with slaves and does not demur in confessing to her early prejudice against the slave population, which she has since transcended. Thus she places herself on the same moral footing as slaves: "Contrary to my intention, I became a constant hearer. There were no young persons, that I knew of, who were in Society at this time, that were not Slaves; on this, and some other accounts, I proudly held out as long as I could, from wholly joining them, tho' I gain'd admittance to many of the private meetings."[30]

She ends with an explosive denunciation of a certain dimension of abolition, difficulty experienced by female slaves in the "forming of their connections":

> You know Sir, that very, very few are brought up with any sense of decency or regard to reputation; with respect to the forming of their connections. They are obliged to be governed more by convenience than affection and being bound by no Laws human or divine, their engagements are easily broken. It is mostly the case that when Female Slaves are raised to wealth, and consequence (may I not say respectability) it is by entering into that way of Life, that cause women in another sphere to fall into disgrace and contempt, I mean concubinage. Of this you have many Instances. Truly labour and want are not the evils of Slavery (horrid system!) though these, as well as the Oppressor's Yoke, cause many still to groan.[31]

This issue of female sexuality in the light of forced concubinage, a notorious and commonly practiced phenomenon, is one to which Elizabeth Hart Thwaites returns more than once, always couching the matter in uncontroversial terms since sexuality is a taboo subject in black female discourse. Put simply, part of discussing abolition is indicting social practices that hamper the lives of black women, especially the disrespect with which their sexuality is treated:

> I will give you one instance out of a thousand, by which you will see they are not allowed many privileges above the beasts that perish. During the Conference [District-Meeting] before the last, a black woman in the Society went with her husband one evening to hear Dr. Coke preach. When the meeting was over, seeing some of the noble crowding the gates with their implements of mischief, with fear and trembling she stole her husband's arm, which was no sooner observed by the gentlemen and ladies (so called), than she was as much ridiculed and abused for doing that which would have appeared strange in them not to do, as though she had committed a crime: the poor affrighted creature withdrew from her husband, to stop the clamour of this narrow-hearted *gentry*, and made haste out of the way. Considering all things that respect this people, I stood amazed that so

50

much conjugal, paternal, and filial affection remains among even the irreligious part of them.   (Hart, "Letter," p. 13)

Moreover, like her sister, Elizabeth Hart Thwaites is unafraid to express her condemnation of the white community and, by contrast, suggests a revision of received opinion on differential morality. In a letter to her cousin Miss Lynch, she evinces her concern about two children, referred to only by their initials, P.O. and M.M., and indirectly combats white discriminatory attitudes and values:

> Many of the children are truly benefitted by religious instruction. I will give you an instance in P.O., the white orphan, who has to beg at the grog-shops, &c. I asked her, a few days ago, how her "mother," as she calls her, was: she answered with tears in her eyes, "She is very poorly, Ma'am, getting worse; but she don't pray; and when I beg her to pray to God, she swears at me."—M.M. is about eleven or twelve years old; you would hardly think, from the modesty and rectitude of her behavior, that she lived in a house of ill-fame, the resort of the basest characters. Her mother, at present having no rest to the soles of her feet, and being miserably poor withal, sends every day to get her meal from a wealthy woman, of the most vulgar manners, who lives with Commissary D.[32]

Men and women of all races are equal; complexion and illegitimate force—the visible signifiers of difference—alone separate them. Elizabeth Hart Thwaites underscores the constant brutalization that diminishes any individual's natural capacity in her refusal to countenance any argument that God intended Africans to be slaves because they are lesser people (Hart, "Letter," p. 14). She exempts only slaveowners with misgivings from her scathing comment—perhaps an escape clause for her slave-owning father. Africans may not be aware of their practices but she ominously pronounces the following:

> It does not suit me to say the worst I know concerning it [the situation of slaves]: only I assure you it comprises a mystery of

iniquity, and endless list of complicated ills, which it is not likely you will ever know. You will not, perhaps, find the sufferers disposed to complain of their case. Not many are capable of *explaining,* however, keenly they may *feel,* their disadvantages.

As to the opposite part, while blinded by self-interest, (and who among them are not more or less so?) they will not allow that they act unjustly. As I do not think it possible that those whose property consists in slaves can be persons of *clean hands,* must I not think you feel something on this account? And particularly for those who are dear to me, that have been so unfortunate as to gain this wretched pre-eminence. Those of them that are any way enlightened are themselves uncomfortable, and would be extricated. They are unhappy at their deviation from the golden rule. "Whatsoever ye would men should do unto you, even so do ye unto them."   (Hart, "Letter," p. 14)

In the process she indicts both white Europeans and creoles: "From all I can learn of them, according to their light, though barbarous and uncivilized, they are not so depraved as the generality of the Europeans, but more especially the West Indians."[33]

However, Elizabeth Hart Thwaites (with her husband Charles) was renowned as the instigator of an educational system for slaves throughout the East Caribbean islands. The acknowledged "superior condition" of Antiguan slaves in 1833 was later attributed not only to the absence of an apprenticeship period following emancipation and the attention of missionaries but specifically to the work of the Thwaites.[34]

In a word, education became Elizabeth Hart's life work. Although a systematic chronology is not available, it seems clear that her classes began around 1798 when Anne Hart married John Gilbert and asked her younger sister to assume responsibility for the classes. When Elizabeth Hart Thwaites records the *History of Methodism* for the Reverend Pattison, she draws attention to the pain she feels about the double standard she had exercised toward her pupils: her own hypocrisy in teaching slaves morality while not practicing what she preached. Slaves, she affirms, lived virtuous lives long before she morally caught up with them: "I met a Class of young women who were Slaves and to whom I said nothing of my then experience, which, when at the worst, did not prevent my enforcing upon them the necessity of a present Salvation. I abated in nothing my severity against Sin, and continually enjoined upon them to avoid the very appearance of evil. Most of these are still in the good way."[35] She comments further on these classes: "Having to meet upwards of 160 in Class, affords me an opportunity of knowing several who have a hearing ear, and understanding heart, two of them are Whites who have a saving knowledge of the truth, the others are Black and Coloured from 13 to 60 years of age."[36]

More concretely, the pidgin English that she attributed to one slave speaker embeds some sense of suppressed cultural bonding and an admonition to any white readers: Institutionalized discrimination is causing moral strife.[37] Once again she employs an argument that ties inappropriate behavior to socioeconomic conditions. Quite simply, slavery causes human degradation at all levels:

Some of the poor Africans can particularize such parts of a Sermon as they felt most, and one of them told me a few Sundays ago, after Preaching, "Massa open me poor sinner heart. He tell me every thing me do," with many of such expressions. I rejoice in the certainty that there are many real converts in St Johns, both of young and Old. I am inclined to think, that one reason why so many of the poor Slaves upon the Estates, cause you trouble and discouragement is, that they are in general received into the Society, as Catechumens, and not convinced Sinners, and if a genuine work of Grace does not take place, they soon relapse into those Sins, which habit and custom have rendered in their meat and drink, particularly Quarreling and Un-chastity.[38]

Elizabeth Hart's commitment to education enables her to talk at length, though indirectly, about gender and race differences; the discourse on education enables her to attack ideas about white superiority. For one thing, a common proslavery allegation denied intellect to Africans. By contrast Hart argues that environment is key:

> There are likewise others [slaves] who, being endued [endowed] with good natural understanding, aspire after refinement, useful knowledge, and sweets of social life, &c., &c.,: were there a possibility of changing the colour of their skins, and emancipating them, with culture they would become ornaments to society. These are not permitted to emerge; they are bound down by some unenlightened, mercenary mortal, who perhaps has not a thought or wish above scraping money together. You may suppose such slaves find it a galling yoke.[39]

In 1809 both sisters were involved in a momentous spiritual and political undertaking. In September of that year they jointly opened the first Caribbean Sunday School for boys and girls, without regard to class or race: "Many [slave children] came from neighbouring estates; it was the first institution of the kind formed in the West Indies, and was formed at a time, too, when teaching slaves to read was so unpopular and suspicious a measure, that the missionaries were instructed [by the London hierarchy] to avoid it, lest it should prevent their admission into places where they might otherwise be allowed to preach the Gospel."[40] Put another way, under the guise of education both sisters did what Methodist missionaries not only were afraid but also were forbidden to do. Additionally, Elizabeth Hart Thwaites's commitment to education went well beyond the establishment of Sunday schools. At some point she visited Montserrat to determine how the Lancastrian system of education worked.[41] In England Joseph Lancaster and Andrew Bell had "mapped out factory methods of teaching . . . By division of labour, student monitors were to funnel instruction for a single teacher to the pupils."[42] Along with her husband she introduced that innovative system to the town of English Harbour.[43]

By 1813 she and her husband had met with teachers and 500 children from neighboring plantations on the estate belonging to the Lyon family and had instituted a plan to teach the children to read. To facilitate this project slaves voluntarily built a schoolroom within six weeks halfway between English Harbour, where the Thwaites lived, and the Lyon estate. She named it Bethesda and taught some 200 to 300 children and adults daily.[44] Her contemporary, Antiguan cultural historian Frances Lanaghan, chronicles a fascinating vignette of Charles and Elizabeth Thwaites at work; the scene exemplifies Elizabeth Hart Thwaites's determination to help usher into existence an educated black populace: "As regards the population of this town . . . [Bridgetown or Willoughby Bay, Antigua] I can give but little information. [I saw] . . . the very kindhearted superintendant of the Wesleyan schools, Mr. Charles Thwaites, and his equally amiable wife, their very pretty little boy, one or two domestics, and their scholars of every shade."[45] Lanaghan goes on to describe the schoolroom, presumably not the earlier one built by slaves:

> After resting for a short time at the superintendant's dwelling, we proceeded to the school-room, a most commodious apartment, measuring 50 ft. by 48 ft., and capable of containing 50 persons. The whole of this establishment, including the superintendant's house, which is detached, was erected by the Church Missionary Society; but after being used by them for a short time, it was turned over to the "Ladies Society," to whom it still belongs, although the Wesleyan Mission holds its school there.
>
> The school-room was but thinly attended upon the day of our visit, there not being more than 40 children—the usual number is about 100. Upon our entrance, they all rose up with "We'll make our obeisance together, as children ought to do," and then, quitting their raised seats, formed into double lines, their teacher at their head, and marched round the apartment to the tune of one of their infant rhymes. After performing many martial-like evolutions, they finally arranged themselves into a deep phalanx, and thus sang another of their little songs.[46]

In Elizabeth Hart's correspondence with her cousin Frances Lynch, she indicates a broader context in which she views education, perhaps one to which Frances Lanaghan, an establishment spokeswoman, was not privy: she sees it as a strategy to gain employment for slaves. Since forced and free labor is the exclusive signifier of a slave, this amounts to an emancipationist statement:

> We have ten girls learning to write. I ought in course to have observed to you that Mr. Thwaites has for some time past been so concerned about the poor children, that he has begged me, if possible, to get myself taught to make lace or any thing that I could teach the girls; and he has been trying to manufacture the long straw into hats for him to teach them; but he made no hand of it.
>
> We have the happiness to see many bidding fair to be valuable and good women, who would probably by this time have been tending their steps to infamy and woe. But what would have been the use of schools, books, teachers, lectures, &c., had not a few benevolent hands been stretched out to enable the poor little creatures.[47]

At Elizabeth Hart's death one of her eulogists documented her life-long devotion to education, her pupils principally being African-Caribbean children and adults, frequently females. At the end the eulogist also quietly reminded the audience how Elizabeth Hart's reputation was slandered as a result of her efforts to educate slaves in the community and neighboring estates:

> She had been from early life engaged with an elder sister in educating a numerous family of younger brothers and sisters; and, not satisfied with communicating knowledge to these primary objects of their attention, they extended it to the slaves of their father's household and estate, by teaching them to read, and inculcating the principles of revealed religion. Mrs. Thwaites afterwards assisted this sister in forming and conducting the first Sunday-school ever established in these Colonies, since it was established more than twenty-four years ago. Not long after, in conjunction with him who now survives to lament her loss, a system of instruction was begun on estates in the country, which afterwards became extensive under the auspices of the Church

Missionary Society, by which they were at length employed, so much so that sixty-one estates had teaching regularly established on them, and two thousand children and youths were brought under instruction at one period. When circumstances not necessary to be here detailed compelled the Church Missionary Society to withdraw from this useful field of labour, Mr. and Mrs. Thwaites were engaged in the service of the Wesleyan Missionary Society and lately, under the kind and liberal patronage of the Ladies' Negro Education Society, commenced a new and delightful branch of instruction,—that of training infants in the way they should go. Mrs. Thwaites' influence, and its beneficial effects on the young females of her charge, can never, when considered in connexion with eternity, be sufficiently appreciated in this delusive world. Suffice it to say, that, being defamed, she endured it; and that her record is on high, and her reward with her God.[48]

Elizabeth Hart's most strident act concerning slavery, however, concerned the eulogist's tactful reference to defamation; it was not an act of her own making but one that demonstrated the fear of emancipation in Antigua. Before the passage of the emancipation bill in 1833, slaves rioted over the suppression of Sunday markets.[49] The island was becoming volatile, political sentiments highly charged. The activities of the Methodists were highly suspect, especially since missionaries were often encoded by the white ruling class as the instigators of revolt because (as their bias dictated) slaves could not organize a rebellion by themselves.

Along with Moravian missionaries and Joseph Phillips, secretary to the Moravians and the only white member of the Moravians in Antigua, Elizabeth Hart Thwaites was called to testify before a committee of the House of Assembly, since she had disbursed funds to those in need. Like Elizabeth Hart Thwaites, Joseph Phillips was a staunch and also a much hated abolitionist, the subject of censure for his marriage to an African-Caribbean woman. Elizabeth Thwaites responded to questions and mentioned those cases she had occasionally relieved. However, she apparently refused to "name the estates, the proprietors, the slaves, the kind of relief, whether money, clothes, or food."[50] In her journal she records her reaction to the end of the proceedings: "We came home very late and tired, and committed ourselves to Him who judgeth righteously, and in confidence that He will be with us and deliver us. Our sleep was refreshing. As I awoke, the path of duty in this matter seemed to open before me, and Mr. Thwaites and I had one view on the subject; and it is comfortable to think that we were under the Divine direction."[51]

After the case was tacitly adjourned, she pursued her activities without hindrance from planters, although she became the target of proslavery ire in the British press. James Macqueen, the editor of the *Glasgow Courier,* cast serious aspersions against both Joseph Phillips and Elizabeth Thwaites in the November 1831 volume of *Blackwoods Magazine.* Macqueen's lengthy attack chronicles how much Elizabeth Thwaites's opposition to slavery had scandalized proslaveryites on both sides of the Atlantic:

> In his [Joseph Phillips'] capacity as second secretary to the deluding society entitled, "The Society for the Relief of Old Worn-out and Diseased Slaves," the Assembly of Antigua, in the name of the colony he had unjustly attacked and basely caluminated, thus speak of him in the Report of their Committee appointed to examine into his charges against the colony:—"Previously to dismissing his evidence, your committee cannot help remarking upon the character of this *second* secretary of the Society, which unfortunately ranks equally low with that of the former one, so much so, *as scarcely to leave a worse in the whole community!!"*
>
> Time, space, and circumstances, compel me to quit this miserable tool [Joseph Phillips] of anti-colonial faction and rancour, and his bosom crony, *Mrs. Thwaites. . . .*
>
> By tools like Mary Prince and Joseph Phillips, [the antislaveryites] mislead and irritate this country, browbeat the Government, and trample upon, as they are permitted to trample upon, our most important transmarine possessions, the value and importance of which I am bound to shew to your Lordship and the public.[52]

Mounting a collective assault against the old colonial order, Anne Hart Gilbert and Elizabeth Hart Thwaites usher in emancipation and counterhegemonic values about black-white relations. As free women of color in Antigua they occupied a special kind of niche, marginalized as women and as Methodists in a colonial taxonomy that configured them in that special category designated as free colored people.[53] The Hart sisters' texts suggest that they strove for a spiritual and tranquil inner life and a self-disciplined external life dedicated to civil and spiritual duties. Their subscription to evangelical Methodism, their enactment of good works, rendered them spiritually inviolate. Assuming the role of educators, teaching slaves to read, and being actively useful in their cultural community was living a Christian life. Religious outsiders themselves, they constantly negotiated from different marginal positions. Female members of well-read black Methodist families who provided affidavits of religious faith for the church fathers, the Hart sisters were acutely aware of their sociosexual profiles and their spiritual equality with whites. That doctrinal egalitarianism, however, did not translate into cultural equality. Even as free women of color, they were linked ethnically to "heathen" Africans and thus occupied a much lower place than whites in the social hierarchy.

Yet that spiritual space of equality concurrently afforded them an incomparable outlet for personal and public advancement and opposition established hegemonic norms. As evangelical women they could represent themselves as Caribbean counterparts of white Methodist women, as educators who epitomized respectability. In a broader context their work was also linked to the contemporary upsurge of evangelical women's activities in England, especially in the nineteenth century when doctrinal differences that separated Methodists and Anglicans had partially dissolved.[54] As high-ranking Methodists the Hart sisters knew of this recent, energetic female intervention in the British emancipation movement. But their motivation to engage in such undertakings had even more complex roots. Not only were religious pursuits liberating in a physical and psychological sense but they also helped to nullify their allegedly inferior status as black Antiguan women.

Hence their texts brim over with a recognition of inequities and their Christ-like compassion toward "lost souls," their strong sense of identification with African-Caribbean men, women, and children. Perhaps there is even a suppressed anger in not being published, a frustration that inflects their texts about the enclosed messages that cannot be overtly heard. Their texts, then, reply to all the anti-intellectual aspersions cast against any African-Caribbeans, including themselves, and lay responsibility for any deficiency or degradation at the feet of the colonial order. They represent the conscious chronicling of a heritage, while revealing a clash of epistemologies and an array of interpretive strategies with which they respond to conflictual situations.

Moreover, both sisters remained keenly aware of the unfair situation of black women in the arena of sexual relations. Black women in a sense could not win. Proslaveryites branded them harlots or temptresses who sexually indulged themselves at will; emancipationists saw black women as innocent victims, all morally degraded and without a shred of an innate seemly modesty. In a colonial society in which males vastly outnumbered females, white men in diverse positions of power were expected to and did keep black women as concubines. Abusive sexual practices (at the hands of white men) were used, too, to underwrite the alleged instability of black family units. In deference to an avowed moral sensibility toward women in general, Foreign Secretary George Canning introduced separate legislation in the British Parliament to stop female flogging and uphold the modesty of black women. The Hart sisters strove to convert young females, not simply to eliminate sexual predation and free up their lives but to give them a chance to be more socially mobile as they themselves were. They saw their social superiors as self-indulgent accomplices in such practices as prostitution, gambling, and public drunkenness for which slaves were generally charged with sole responsibility. The sisters wanted to change the withering away of the spirit caused by these practices.

Anne Hart Gilbert and Elizabeth Hart Thwaites seem to have taken Frances Lanaghan's concern to heart when she stated: "Slaves and free black females were often expected to become the mistresses of white men."[55] Their professional lives were spent trying to dissolve that near certainty. The timing of the Sunday schools was important since it followed a call by Thomas Coke that specifically denounced the San Domingo Revolution: "It is to the gospel, that Great Britain in all probability, stands indebted for the preservation of many of her richest colonial possessions, even to the present day: that her swarthy subjects have not revolted like those of a neighbouring island; and committed those depredations on the white inhabitants, which humanity shudders to name."[56]

It seems unlikely that the sisters saw the revolution from the Reverend Thomas Coke's viewpoint. It was more likely than not that the Methodist bureaucracy would adopt a more pacific posture than Wesley's. Although Antigua was the "mother-island of the West Indian Methodism" from the start of evangelizing missions, Methodist missionaries shied from advocating emancipation overtly, since they were already regarded suspiciously as outsiders.[57] They were keenly aware of their own role as upholders of the faith and mothers of spirituality, legitimate public authorities. Upheld by their spiritual knowledge that the imago dei resided in every individual, that all people, but for historical circumstances, were politically and culturally equal, Anne Hart Gilbert and Elizabeth Hart Thwaites stressed the power of the word and the need for literacy. The sisters' view of Antiguan society meshed with their sense of themselves as educators; since they shared a vision of a post-emancipation society, their concern was practical as well as spiritual. They saw the need for all African-Caribbeans to fit into Antiguan society and be members of the wider community. If former slaves could not read and offered no skills in a transformed market economy, the sisters knew, their chance of survival was diminished; thus their push for literacy and vocational skills. They wanted all African-Caribbeans to have an appropriately worthwhile place in future society; hence their concerted efforts to educate black adults as well as children and to dissolve attempts by whites to create distance between themselves and the black population, freed like themselves, or enslaved.[58] Through their texts and actions the sisters performed radical surgery on the Antiguan body politic.

In fact Elizabeth Thwaites and her sister were implicitly threatening the Methodist male hegemony with the establishment of a break-away church. In a much publicized religious action in the United States, Absalom Jones, a former slave who was insulted by bigoted Methodist institutional practices, had established the African Methodist Episcopal Church in 1793 with other angry black freed men and women. Throughout their writings the sisters sound an intertextual echo of a comparable, religious separatism.

As subalterns with complex subjectivities, they were determined to speak, assuming roles on a tightrope of acceptability. They declined to be situated in any prescribed colonizing space for free colored women. Instead they carved out for themselves an ambiguous niche that elevated their status not only as African-Caribbean women but as political activists and social workers. They fabricate as well as embrace personas and subjectivities that make resistance possible.[59] Through their activities and social positions, they canceled conventional stigmas attached to a free colored status. After all, they were focusing on Methodism and education, the ne plus ultra of emerging lower-class identity. Most particularly they dissipated the negative connotations associated with free black women. Given the fact that their piety precluded them from any potential (and customary) designation as "loose" women, they were expanding the definition of middle-class respectability. Their conscious transcendence of such roles unsettled the very designations themselves; they helped to dissolve colonial coding based on abuse and expropriation of black female bodies. To put the matter another way, Anne Hart Gilbert and Elizabeth Hart Thwaites split the usually conflated gendered and colonial spaces reserved for free colored women. As black women they insisted on an individual and moral status.

Navigating between two modalities—spiritual conformity as Christians and their abolitionist self-fashioning—they constructed images of themselves that sabotaged and subverted. In most of their work they undermined or reversed dominant ideology. Representing slaves as educable and smart, they unpacked centuries-old stereotypes, vindicating codings of both the free colored and the slave population. In that sense they became representatives of slaves and free colored people alike.

In other words, they used to the advantage of slaves and female slaves in particular the fact that they were educators at a time of rapid expansion in the Methodist Society. It gave them leeway and opportunities for creative strategies of resistance. Unlike their white counterparts they were less likely to think that "savagery" was "out there."[60] Instead of catering to old stereotypes of slaves as infantilized human beings—a designation that affirmed and perpetuated metropolitan as well as Antiguan colonial power—they subverted these centuries-old formulae. They configured slaves as people like themselves who lacked circumstances and opportunities. Their texts stopped the isolation of freed (or enslaved) Africans as people with no rights. Indirectly they "reveal[ed] their political usefulness and . . . len[t] themselves to economic profit."[61] The pivotal presence of those texts effectively altered the material context and its power relations.

The sisters' tireless domestic missionary work can be seen in another light in Frantz Fanon's conceptualizations. Aware of their constructed inferior status they channeled repressed anger into counterinsistences, mimicking and otherwise.[62] Since they could not speak prejudice out loud, could scarcely even name it publicly, they inscribed it into their instruction of black children.

The sisters, then, write from the edges as a way of coping with their psychic and cultural fragmentation. But these borders are not visible borders. They are nuanced actions, textual silences, quiet rebuttals that exist while the sisters simultaneously maintain a relatively visible position in the nonconformist community.

By thematizing concerns they had as black Antiguans while

foregrounding the occupiers' religion, they established a specific black Antiguan Methodist cultural identity. In their unity of sorts with indigenous culture they foreshadowed and even helped precipitate an end to Antiguan powerlessness vis-à-vis white Europeans. A sense of black self-determination and a future emancipation—however inchoate and faint—induced innovation, experimentation, and even self-fabrication disguised as spiritual orthodoxy.

Religious outsiders themselves, they represent slaves and other black Antiguans to the white community while simultaneously seeking conversion. Expressing new human possibilities for African-Caribbeans, their writings allude to several abolitionist texts, including William Cowper's poems and Wilberforce's parliamentary speeches. Representing a silenced class of people usually relegated to the borders, these two women capitulated to no one and introduced new cultural scripts that established complex dialogue within their own society and with posterity.

Mansfield Park:
Plantocratic Paradigms

> The remembrance . . . of what she had suf-
> fered in being torn from them, came over her
> with renewed strength, and it seemed as if to
> be at home again, would heal every pain that
> had since grown out of the separation.
>
> —Jane Austen,
> *Mansfield Park,* p. 364

As a Jacobin concerned with women's rights in 1792, Mary Wollstonecraft argues for a greater distribution of political power in
Britain. As antislavery evangelical Methodists writing in Antigua
from the 1790s until the 1830s, Anne Hart Gilbert and Elizabeth
Hart Thwaites also argue for a greater distribution of power and a
special attentiveness to the condition of African-Caribbean women.
Unlike Jane Austen's political conservatism, however, they do not
aim to legitimize the ruling class in Antigua. To push the contrary
argument as far as it can go, the Hart sisters seek obliquely to

subvert the colonial order under the guise of evangelical activities. At another level the Hart sisters resemble Jane Austen, some of whose later spiritual beliefs are ventriloquized through Fanny Price.

On the other hand, in a Eurocentric, post-abolition narrative Jane Austen wants to legitimize the ruling class in light of the French Revolution while critiquing gender relations; she further posits a world of humanitarian interactions between Antiguan slaveowners and slaves. As such, following the successful passage of the Abolition Bill in 1807, *Mansfield Park* initiates a new chapter in colonialist fiction. It also illuminates an Antiguan ruling-class world that is rarely fleshed out or even referred to in the texts of Anne Hart Gilbert and Elizabeth Hart Thwaites. Although the novel works against the idea of the traditionally closed and brutal world of plantocratic relations, it nonetheless entertains the option of emancipation—as opposed to abolition—only through the sound of muffled rebel voices. In order to stage a future society peaceably perpetuating British rule, Jane Austen transforms Sir Thomas Bertram of Mansfield Park—who is also a plantation owner in Antigua—from a characteristically imperious "West Indian" planter—stock figure of ridicule in contemporary drama, poetry, and novels—into a benevolent, reforming landowner.[1] Nonetheless, as Toni Morrison argues in another context in *Playing in the Dark,* Sir Thomas garners a different kind of authority in Antigua from that of the Hart sisters, one that is defined against the grain of the black population:

> But what had he known before? Fine education, London sophistication, theological and scientific thought. None of these, one gathers, could provide him with the authority and autonomy that Mississippi planter life did. Also this sense is understood to be a force that flows, already present and ready to spill as a result of his "absolute control over the lives of others." This force is not a willed domination, a thought-out, calculated choice, but rather a kind of natural resource, a Niagara Falls waiting to drench Dunbar as soon as he is in a position to assume absolute control. Once he has moved into that position, he is resurrected

as a new man, a distinctive man—a different man. And whatever his social status in London, in the New World he is a gentleman. More gentle, more man. The site of his transformation is within rawness: he is backgrounded by savagery.[2]

Given the state of agitation in the Caribbean in the early 1800s, the unreality of this scenario forces textual contradictions and eruptions. No African-Caribbean people speak, no mention is ever made of slave plots or insurrections, and even slaves' white counterparts—women in rebellion in one form or another—are assimilated or banished.[3] Thus gender relations at home parallel and echo traditional relationships of power between the colonialists and colonized peoples: White British women visibly signify the most egregiously and invisibly repressed of the text—African-Caribbeans themselves. They mark silent African-Caribbean rebels as well as their own disenfranchisement and class and gender victimization.

Let me contextualize these remarks by noting that *Mansfield Park* was begun by Jane Austen in early 1811 and published in 1814, with its novelistic chronology extending from 1808 through 1809. As a result of the energetic abolition movement and parliamentary compromise with the West India lobby in 1792, slaveowners' efforts to resist legal abolition, let alone emancipation, were notorious.[4]

A transatlantic landowner, Sir Thomas Bertram is fictionally characterized as one of those members of Parliament who defended plantocratic interests.[5] He belonged to the outer ring of absentee planters and merchants who never, or rarely, visited the colonies, although their connections remained solid.[6] In Raymond Williams's words:

Important parts of the country-house system, from the sixteenth to the eighteenth centuries, were built on the profits of . . . trade [with the colonies]. Spices, sugar, tea, coffee, tobacco, gold and silver: these fed, as mercantile profits, into an English social order, over and above the profits on English stock and crops. . . . The country-houses which were the apex of a local system of exploitation then had many connections to these distant lands. . . . [Moreover], the new rural economy of the tropical plantations—sugar, coffee, cotton—was built by [the] trade in flesh, and once again the profits fed back into the country-house system: not only the profits on the commodities but . . . the profits on slaves.[7]

After a brief, quiescent period following the passage of the abolition bill in 1807, however, fierce contestations over slavery began anew at home and abroad. As the British press reported news of increasing atrocities in 1809, 1810, and 1811, it became obvious that the abolitionists' utopian vision of a Caribbean plantocracy committed to ameliorating the conditions of their only remaining slaves was transparently false.[8] This rise in atrocities and vigorous illicit trading spurred parliamentary proposals that all Caribbean slaves be registered.[9] Old colonial legislatures, including Antigua's, opposed slave registries on constitutional grounds because such a procedure violated their right of internal taxation; colonialists did not assent until 1820.

In fact, the time during which *Mansfield Park* was written marked a turning point in the fortunes of the gentry, to which social class Sir Thomas, as a baronet, arguably belonged.[10] In England the Luddite riots fomented unrest, the prime minister was assassinated, war was declared against the United States, and the gentry endured a general economic crisis. Mrs. Norris, Sir Thomas's sister-in-law, informs us that Sir Thomas's financial stability depends on maintaining his Caribbean property:[11] his "means will be rather straitened if the Antiguan estate is to make such poor returns."[12] Sir Thomas needs his Caribbean profits to stay afloat financially in England; colonialism underwrites his social and cultural position.

Thus ongoing news of Caribbean economic crises exacerbates Sir Thomas's already straitened circumstances. Sugar prices had plummeted as a result of a major depression after 1807. The ensuing urgency to diversify the imperiled sugar monoculture made the physical presence of customarily absentee landlords expedient,[13] and so Sir Thomas was obliged "to go to Antigua himself, for the

better arrangement of his affairs."[14] The task at hand was to maintain his estates at a profit and, since trading was now illegal, to
ensure in the process the survival of his slaves as steady, well-
nourished workers. Sadistic overseers, with whom Sir Thomas may
have been content in the past (provided returns were satisfactory),
would no longer do. His appearance when he returns to England
suggests not only an exhausting engagement with his overseers and
a severe reaction to noisome conditions but also emphasizes through
metonym his affiliation with the creole class. He "had the burnt,
fagged, worn look of fatigue and a hot climate."[15]

The society to which Sir Thomas traveled was dominated by
aggressive oppositional relations between colonialists and colonized
people, although absentee landlordism was unusual on Antigua
compared to its frequency on neighboring islands. As a near-noble
landowner, Sir Thomas would socialize with the commander-in-
chief of the Leeward Islands, the Right Honorable Ralph, Lord
Lavington, who in "real life" chose to set a constant and pointed
public example of desirable relations between colonizers and colonized:

> His Christmas balls and routs were upon the highest scale of
> magnificence; but he was a great stickler for etiquette, and a firm
> upholder of difference of rank and *colour* [Lanaghan's underlin-
> ing]. . . . He would not upon any occasion, receive a letter or
> parcel from the fingers of a black or coloured man, and in order
> to guard against such *horrible defilement,* he had a golden instru-
> ment wrought something like a pair of sugar tongs, with which
> he was accustomed to hold the presented article.[16]

The Anglican ruling-class coterie with whom Sir Thomas associated disapprobated too much spiritual stirring up of slaves, the
very activities in which the Hart sisters were engaged. Lord Lavington's fastidiousness about propriety is consonant with constant efforts to maintain a rigid social and political hierarchy. His phobia
underscores the doughty activities of Anne Hart Gilbert and Elizabeth Hart Thwaites. Back home, abolitionists challenged the con-

doned maltreatment of slaves encapsulated in Lord Lavington's insidious public behavior; they decried the atrocities that his cultural practice validated: violations of the Abolition Act, as well as individual cases of heinous maltreatment and murders of slaves by planters in 1810 and 1811.[17] Since the powerful proslavery lobby indefatigably suppressed these events as far as their power allowed, only those with access to ongoing revelations in the press and through rumor could stay abreast of daily developments. The centuries-long ideological battle over the humanity of Africans constantly and variously manifested itself.

Power relations within the community of Mansfield Park reenact and refashion plantocratic paradigms; those who work for Sir Thomas and his entourage both at home and abroad are locked into hierarchical and abusive patterns of behavior, though under widely different circumstances. The cruel officiousness of protagonist Fanny Price's aunt, Mrs. Norris, who is effectively Sir Thomas's overseer and lives in the suggestively named white house "across the park" from the Great House, underlines his plantocratic style of administration.[18]

Mrs. Norris's surname recalls John Norris, one of the most vile proslaveryites of the day. Austen was well aware of Norris's notoriety, having read Thomas Clarkson's celebrated *History of the Abolition of the Slave Trade* in which Norris is categorically condemned. Clarkson's text was published in 1808 and read by Jane Austen while she was working out the plot of *Mansfield Park*.[19] Not only had Clarkson's history astounded her but she admitted to her sister Cassandra that she had once been "in love" with the famous abolitionist whose devotion, industry, and total lack of regard for his own life in the cause was legend.[20] Clarkson chronicles how Norris represented himself to Clarkson in Liverpool as an opponent of the slave trade, then arrived in London as a proslavery delegate representing Liverpool.[21] After contacting Norris for an explanation, Clarkson notes Norris's unctuously self-serving response: "After having paid high compliments to the general force of my arguments, and the general justice and humanity of my sentiments on this great question, which had made a deep impression upon his mind, he had found occasion to differ from me, since we had last parted, on particular points, and that he had therefore less reluctantly yielded to the call of becoming a delegate,—though notwithstanding he would gladly have declined the office if he could have done it with propriety."[22]

Underscoring the intertextual designation of Mrs. Norris as sadistic overseer, Sir Thomas himself is centerstaged as "master," especially in his treatment of niece Fanny Price. With very little ceremony and offering Fanny Price's family no say in the matter, Sir Thomas and Mrs. Norris engineer the transference of this ten-year-old poor relation from her home in Portsmouth to Mansfield Park. A marginalized, almost despised family, the Prices lose one of their own to accommodate Mrs. Norris's need to appear charitable; Sir Thomas eventually concurs in her decision although he reserves his judgment to return Fanny Price if she threatens domestic stability. Portsmouth, by this account, is the uncivilized other; its members overflow with energies that menace the security of Mansfield Park. Epitomizing the clash of epistemologies in the text, Portsmouth marks a way of living that negates the tightly controlled social order and challenges the sovereign law embodied in Sir Thomas by ignoring it altogether. On the other hand, since Portsmouth as a naval town serves to uphold Sir Thomas's position by enforcing British control of the West Indies, what might be more important in a different way is that in the domestic arena of England, the link between the two must be separated. The expropriated Fanny Price hails from the milieu of transgressors who always signify the target of their activities: kidnapped and captive slaves.

Young Fanny Price's removal from her family is described in terms often reserved for epiphanic moments in the narrative of slavery: "The remembrance . . . of what she had suffered in being torn from them, came over her with renewed strength, and it seemed as if to be at home again, would heal every pain that had since grown out of the separation."[23]

71

This abhorrence of family fracture recalls Elizabeth Hart Thaites's similar opposition to that practice.[24] At the same time, of course, crucial differences exist between Fanny Price's situation and that of bondswomen: material conditions, educational opportunities, the privileges (often dangerously assumed to be normative) of class and of color. While not discounting provocative similarities—Fanny Price does hail from humble origins—Fanny Price can also always exercise choice.

This mercantilist attitude toward human relationships, represented as disinterested benevolence toward Fanny Price, nonetheless invokes traditionally conservative rationales for the "trade in flesh." Family feeling or unity never becomes an issue, since pro-slaveryites do not recognize African and slave families as legally sanctioned and deny their reality. On the contrary, the West Indian lobby argued that bringing slaves to the Caribbean was a good deed, a way of civilizing those whose environment provided them with nothing but barbarism—precisely the same basis for the justification of bringing Fanny Price to Mansfield Park. This is also, let it be noted, the very argument to which the Hart sisters strenuously objected.

So when Fanny arrives at Mansfield Park, she is closely watched for evidence of her uncouth otherness. She must accept Sir Thomas's authority unconditionally or she will be removed. Sir Thomas scrutinizes her "disposition," anticipating "gross ignorance, some meanness of opinions, and very distressing vulgarity of manner."[25] Eventually he decides she has a "tractable disposition, and seemed likely to give them little trouble."[26] She will acclimate well. Nonetheless, his children "cannot be equals [with Fanny Price]. Their rank, fortune, rights, and expectations will always be different."[27]

Fanny herself begins to adapt to the value system at Mansfield, learning "to know their ways, and to catch the best manner of conforming to them." Fanny thinks "too lowly of her own claims" and "too lowly of her own situation" to challenge values that keep her low.[28] Underscoring class difference and alluding to the colonial-sexual nexus, profligate elder son Tom, the heir apparent to

Sir Thomas's colonial enterprise, assures Fanny Price that she can be a "creepmouse" all she wants as long as she obeys his commands.

Just as markedly, when Fanny Price years later is deciding what to wear at the ball, the point of contention is whose chain (or necklace) she will wear. The lurking question is to whom will she subject herself or belong. To what extent has Mansfield Park and its values begun to construct her subjectivity? Gladly she decides on the chain of her future husband, Sir Thomas's younger son, Edmund. Moreover, when Sir Thomas leaves for Antigua, she steps into his moral shoes; she opposes Mrs. Norris's opportunism and informally assumes the role of the "good" overseer, her aunt's alter ego. Mimicking Sir Thomas, willingly cooperating in her own assimilation, she speaks for and through him. Fanny Price helps to foreshadow and map a new colonial landscape that upholds the moral status quo but draws the line at arbitrary judgment and excessive indulgence. In the chapel scene at Sotherton, for instance, Fanny Price identifies herself as an opponent of change with some evangelical leanings.[29] Edmund, on the other hand, underscores Fanny's complicity in her own assimilation when he confides—to her delight—as she leaves for Portsmouth that she will "belong to [them] almost as much as ever."[30]

Yet Fanny Price is still the daughter of Portsmouth—Mansfield Park's relegated other, reared to succeed pluckily against the odds. Her master-slave relationship with Sir Thomas operates on the register of two opposing discourses: complicity and rebellion. Her stalwart refusal to marry Henry Crawford and the punishment of summary banishment she incurs identify Mansfield Park ideologically as an institution that rallies to disempower anyone who jeopardizes Sir Thomas's landed aristocratic reign. This is especially true in the case of the déclassé Fanny Price, to whom Mansfield Park has opened its portals. In return she opposes its patriarchal demands on females as property by claiming one form of independence, thereby rendering herself an unregenerate ingrate in ruling-class eyes. Sir Thomas even describes her in language reserved for slave insurrectionists: "I had thought you peculiarly free from wil-

73

fulness of temper, self-conceit, and every tendency to that independence of spirit, which prevails so much in modern days, even in
young women, and which in young women is offensive and disgust-
ing beyond all common offence. But you have now shewn me that
you can be wilful and perverse."[31]

Nonetheless, Fanny Price's refusal to marry Henry Crawford is
evidence of her agency and autonomy, despite her lowly status in
the family. Slave women would not be offered such a choice when
forced to be breeders and mistresses to white planters. To Sir
Thomas, Fanny Price's feelings are as irrelevant as slaves' feelings;
she is his object. In Tzvetan Todorov's words, "Those who are not
subjects have no desires.[32]

Fanny Price responds to her natal family almost exclusively as an
other after Sir Thomas banishes her to Portsmouth. Such is the
enormity of his ideological power. His risk in sending her to resist
Portsmouth and embrace Mansfield Park values pays off. Her home
is nothing but "noise, disorder, impropriety," her overworked im-
pecunious mother pronounced "a dawdler and a slattern," language
often reserved for slave communities.[33] Portsmouth reconstitutes
Fanny Price as Sir Thomas's transformed daughter, no longer the
exiled object; while at Portsmouth she barricades herself ideologically, as it were, inside Mansfield Park, functioning as its representative. Her mother's features, which she has not seen in over a
decade, endear themselves to her—not because she has missed
seeing them but because they remind Fanny Price of Lady Bertram,
her mother's sister and Sir Thomas's wife: "They brought her Aunt
Bertram's before her."[34] Fanny Price has come to resemble the
Eurocentrically conceived "grateful Negro" in pre-abolition tales
who collaborated with kind owners and discouraged disobedience
among rebel slaves.[35] Her embrace of Mansfield Park's values dissolves any binding association with her family and her old life.

After leaving Portsmouth for the second time, Fanny "was be-
loved" by her adopted family in Mansfield Park, the passive tense
affirming her surrender of agency (p. 461). When Edmund decides
she will make him an appropriate wife, her parents' response is not

mentioned. We assume they are neither told nor invited to the wedding. The only Portsmouth members who textually reappear are the conformists: sister Susan, coded as a second Fanny, ready to satisfy Lady Bertram's need for a round-the-clock assistant, and impeccable sailor-brother William, who exercised "continued good conduct" (p. 462).

Sir Thomas's commercial approach to Fanny Price reformulates the treatment he previously accorded her mother Frances Price, who "disoblig[ed]" her family when she married a lieutenant of marines "without education, fortune, or connections"; as a result, the Mansfield Park inner circle acts almost as if Frances Price senior did not exist; certainly she has no rights as a parent, so her children can be more or less removed at will. The text hints, too, that having ten babies in nine years is tantamount to a reprehensible lack of restraint. Neither Mrs. Price's continuing independence in not seeking help nor her maintenance of a large family on a pittance elicit textual approbation. Rather, she is lucky, in the text's terms, to be the recipient of Sir Thomas's charity. With almost all immediate family ties severed, her status, mutatis mutandi, parallels that of her sister Lady Bertram, whose dowry has doomed her to the borders in a different sense. Within a phallocratic economy their lives elicit contempt and condescension.

Lady Bertram, Mrs. Norris, and Frances Price make up the trio of sisters who collectively display the degradation of colonial-gender relations. In the opening sentence of *Mansfield Park*, which highlights Sir Thomas's hegemonic order, the trope of capture and control that infuses the text first appears: "About thirty years ago, Miss Maria Ward of Huntingdon, with only seven thousand pounds, had the good luck to captivate Sir Thomas Bertram, of Mansfield Park, in the county of Northampton, and to be thereby raised to the rank of a baronet's lady, with all the comforts and consequences of an handsome house and large income."

The text thus describes her alleged initial conquest of Sir Thomas in arrestingly ironic tones and in doing so, as in the famous opening assertion in *Pride and Prejudice*, *Mansfield Park*'s first sentence also celebrates its opposite: Sir Thomas's acquisition of a desirable social object. Maria Ward instantly drops out of sight, both in nomenclature and in self-led behavior. Occupying the role of a slatternly plantation mistress—"she never thought of being useful" (p. 179)— Lady Bertram's prominent class status through marriage collides with the posture of an undermined female. The lap dog upon which she lavishes attention—"no one is to tease my poor pug"—emblemizes her pathetically protected status.[36] When Sir Thomas has to break news to her, he approaches her as he would a child. During his absence she rather tellingly works on "yards of fringe"—appropriate for a marginalized wife—and when he returns, in recognition of her imposed vacuity, she waits to have "her whole comprehension filled by his narratives."[37] She epitomizes emptiness, a vacant object-status, a conditioned subject who commits spiritual suicide.

Only once does a hint of spunky self-respect surface. A momentary ambiguity nags the text when she comments, on Sir Thomas's departure for Antigua, that she does not fear for his safety. Is she overly confident he will be safe because she is oblivious to maritime danger due to the Napoleonic wars? Or does she not care? Does her comment speak unconsciously about her recognition of powerlessness? Does it quietly express repressed anger?

Viewing social fluidity as ambiguous for women (if it could facilitate new opportunities, it could similarly foster disaster), the three adult sisters acutely exemplify its differential impact. Through their representation Jane Austen reaffirms the influence of commercial wealth on social position. Maria Ward marries Sir Thomas Bertram. Frances Ward marries Mr. Ward, a sailor, and bears nine children, while Mrs. Norris's commercial or monetary avarice and insecurity so personally corrupts her that she countenances Maria Bertram's sexual indiscretion. This stark contrast in the sisters' situations silently reminds us of the likely futures of the novel's younger women who engage our imaginations. It points out that conditions of possibility for a satisfying life are gloomy at best.

Sir Thomas's behavior on both sides of the Atlantic signals a plantocratic mode of behavior. Through the trope of his journey to

Antigua, his long absence, and his sparing commentary about his experiences when he returns, Austen stresses his planter-like detachment from humanity or his playing down of the facts, or both. One of the few things he did in Antigua—we learn—is attend a ball in the company of creoles—a term for white planters born in the colonies that became a term of derision in the eighteenth and nineteenth centuries; culturally and economically, Sir Thomas is inextricably linked to his Antiguan counterparts. Once again Sir Thomas is culturally and economically worlds apart from the evangelical Hart sisters who would deplore the dancing as devil's work. And given certain much touted facts about planters, contemporaries could have amplified Sir Thomas's character in a way that would expressively inflect Lady Bertram's remark about not being concerned about his safety. Planters were infamous for taking slave mistresses and fathering children.

Edward Long, who wrote the popular *History of Jamaica* (1774), describes creole activities as follows:

> Creole men . . . are in general sensible, of quick apprehension, brave, good-natured, affable, generous, temperate, and sober; unsuspicious, lovers of freedom, fond of social enjoyments, tender fathers, humane and indulgent masters; firm and sincere friends, where they once repose a confidence; their tables are covered with plenty of good cheer . . . ; their hospitality is unlimited . . . ; they affect gaiety and diversions, which in general are cards, billiards, backgammon, chess, horse-racing, hog-hunting, shooting, fishing, dancing, and music. . . . With a strong natural propensity to the other sex, they are not always the most chaste and faithful of husbands.[38]

Furthermore, Lowell Joseph Ragatz points out that from the mid eighteenth century, white fathers generously, frequently, and privately provided for "illegitimate half-breed children" despite laws prohibiting the transmission of substantial property to blacks:

> The number of free persons of color in Barbados, largely recruited through illicit relations with white men and negresses,

rose from 448 to 2,229 between 1768 and 1802, while the number in Dominica soared from 600 in 1773 to more than 2,800 in 1804. This rapid growth of a mixed blood element in the British West Indies after 1750 arose chiefly from the Anglo-Saxon's now merely transitory residence there and the small number of white women remaining in the islands. Concubinage became well-nigh universal in the second half of the eighteenth century and the system pervaded all ranks of society. During the administration of Governor Ricketts in Barbados in the 1790's, a comely negress even reigned at government house, enjoying all a wife's privileges save presiding publicly at his table.[39]

According to August Kotzebue's well-known play, *Lovers' Vows*, which the characters in *Mansfield Park* choose to rehearse for their recreation, no love/lust exists in England, only "in all barbarous countries."[40] Austen uses this play to intertextualize the characters' motives and interactions. A remark from the play's philandering Count Cassel that comments on sexual exploitation in the Caribbean matches contemporary accounts and illuminates the character of Sir Thomas.[41]

Jane Austen was well aware of these infamous activities. She knew about the estate of the Nibbs family in Antigua because the Reverend George Austen, her father, was a trustee; she also knew of the Nibbs's "mulatto" relative. As one critic concretely contends: "Jane Austen would certainly have been aware of the likelihood of a family such as her fictional Bertrams having numerous mulatto relatives in Antigua."[42] The Hart sisters oppose these practices and try to compensate for them through their literacy program and the Female Refuge Society. Sir Thomas's condemnation of Mrs. Price's marrying low and his anger at Fanny Price's refusal to accommodate him by marrying Henry Crawford mocks planters' infamous, quotidian practices.

A question then crops up: Does Sir Thomas banish his daughter Maria and censure Henry Crawford because their sexual indulgences mirror his Antiguan conduct? Is one dimension of his behavior a form of self-projection, an unconscious denial of his dual and contradictory realities in the Caribbean and Britain?

Another victim of Sir Thomas's mercantilist attitudes, elder daughter Maria refuses to be Lady Bertram's clone. Instead she stands with her exiled Aunt Frances and cousin Fanny in claiming sexual independence. Her actions are even more morally outré since she has already been manipulated into marriage with Rushworth, a man whom her father desires financially. For example, in the gate scene at Sotherton Maria symbolically and literally refuses to be imprisoned. Maria, that is, falls for the ideological trap that is set for her and is punished for trying to release herself.[43] Mary Crawford, who also disregards Sir Thomas's authority and is coded as a predator of sorts, similarly wrestles for personal autonomy and is configured as more evil because she disregards Sir Thomas's values. Linked by their given names, they are different versions of a gendered bid for identity.[44]

In the text's terms none of these spirited acts by women in multiple postures of subjection can be vindicated except that of the conflicted Fanny Price. The Crawfords are reduced to the social margins, Henry for visible rakishness, Mary for "evil" and bold collaboration in her brother's escapades. The possibility smolders that Sir Thomas cannot contain an English reflection of his Antiguan self. He represents men who control the general slave population, and the female slave population in particular, through varieties of abuse. When women like Frances and Fanny Price, Maria Bertram, and Mary Crawford articulate a counterdiscourse against their objectification, Sir Thomas stands firm. Insurgent women become deleted subjects, objects of his wrath who must be appropriately punished, usually for keeps. At the conscious and unconscious level, the text continually inscribes challenges to the assumed inferiority of women and the right of a hegemonic patriarch to use women as he pleases.

Most systematically of all, however, *Lovers' Vows* intertextualizes property-owning attitudes that characterize planter-slave relations, including Sir Thomas's flagrant neglect of female welfare.[45] At the same time the dramatic resolution of these corrupt interrelationships appears to exonerate Sir Thomas and validate patriarchal rule. Clearly coded as Sir Thomas, the Baron is multiply conflicted. In former days he had abandoned naïve and pregnant Agnes, who bore Frederick, thus validating the reputation of *Lover's Vows* as a "byword for moral and social subversion."[46] Like the "deserted and neglected negroes" of Antigua who will become a later focus of national concern, Agnes is now starving to death and homeless. Eventually, however, the Baron's callous desertion is mitigated by information that he has hired helpers to search constantly till they find her. In the end the Baron decides to marry Agnes, though he fails to consult her about his plan. Like Maria Ward she is assumed to desire such a splendid match.

In like manner the Baron's efforts to marry off his daughter Amelia to silly Count Cassel are soon revealed as nonbinding. When he learns that Amelia loves Pastor Anhalt, the Baron readily consents, a scenario that comments on the marital imbroglio of Fanny Price, Henry Crawford, and Edmund Bertram. The case of Frederick, who strikes the Baron in the course of trying to save his mother's life, allusively invokes the nature of Sir Thomas's power: the Baron orders Frederick killed even though "a child might have overpowered him," for "to save him would set a bad example."[47] Only when the Baron discovers that Frederick is his son does parental feeling induce him to relent. In doing so the Baron earns permission to be readmitted to the human community. Feudal laws and relations in *Lovers' Vows* sign those of the plantocracy. In using the play in this way Austen signals the possible illegitimacy of colonial relations because she knows that feudal relations have been abolished in England. She is not opposing all forms of authority. But she is, however, concerned about validating authority—about naming illegitimate authority precisely to bolster legitimate authority.

Mansfield Park initiated a new chapter in colonialist fiction as old and new abolitionists came to terms with the fact that the Abolition Bill did not fulfill its minimum requirement—amelioration of inhuman conditions. Jane Austen's repugnance for the slave trade, moreover, is well documented—her brother Francis was a vigorous

abolitionist—and by the time she writes *Emma* in 1816 her condemnation is forthright.[48]

In the later novel the issue of the slave trade arises during a
conversation between Jane Fairfax and Mrs. Elton over the former's
finding suitable employment:

> "Excuse me, ma'am, but this is by no means my intention; I
> make no inquiry myself, and should be sorry to have any made
> to my friends. When I am quite determined as to the time, I am
> not at all afraid of being long unemployed. There are places in
> town, offices, where inquiry would soon produce something—
> Offices for the sale—not quite of human flesh—but of human
> intellect."
>
> "Oh! my dear, human flesh! You quite shock me; if you mean
> a fling at the slave-trade, I assure you Mr. Suckling was always
> rather a friend to the abolition."
>
> "I did not mean, I was not thinking of the slave-trade,"
> replied Jane; "governess-trade, I assure you, was all that I had in
> view; widely different certainly as to the guilt of those who carry
> it on; but as to the great misery of the victims, I do not know
> where it lies."[49]

By 1816 Jane Austen is making much more overt connections
between the situation of slaves and white Englishwomen.[50] She
removes the discussion from Antigua, a very specific locale in the
East Caribbean with which her family has connections, and applies
it generally. Notably, however, she does not champion emancipation. She advocates abolition of the slave trade, an interim, less
radical demand that attracted more supporters.

Hence Sir Thomas's chastening is one way of prescribing this
letting-up process among a seemingly unregenerate plantocracy. He
reconstitutes himself as a moral rather than a profit-oriented planter,
a condition inveterately resisted among the colonial ruling class.
Recent experiences in the House of Commons as well as the Caribbean have persuaded Sir Thomas, Jane Austen subtly argues, that
the old order may be doomed and disappearing. As a member of

Parliament, Sir Thomas would have been witnessing at first hand the efforts of Wilberforce and his supporters to initiate corrective legislation. In admitting his errors and curbing his selfishness, Sir Thomas comes to represent the liberal-conservative ideal of humanitarian plantation ownership at a time when outright manumission is effectively a nonissue.

It hardly seems to be a coincidence that *Mansfield Park* echoes the name of Lord Chief Justice Mansfield, who wrote the legal decision for the James Somerset case in 1772. The decision stipulated that no slaves could be forcibly returned from Britain to the Caribbean, which was widely interpreted to mean that slavery in Britain had been legally abolished.[51] Austen's invocation of Lord Mansfield's name—with its echo, of *emancipation*—suggests the novel's intrinsic engagement with slavery and a view of Sir Thomas's plantations as a place where master-slave relations are beginning to dissolve.[52] To underscore that point, the word *plantation* is frequently used to denote Sir Thomas's property on both sides of the Atlantic.

At another level the allusion to Lord Mansfield's ruling warns and censures all those who try to further impose their will on the already subjugated—in Sir Thomas's case, Fanny Price and by extension his Antiguan slaves. The choice of Mans field for the title underscores the idea of property in the hands of a patriarch— one man's plantations—and in its compression of several frames of meaning and reference, it connects the Caribbean plantation system and its master-slave relationships to tyrannical gender relations at home and abroad.

Jane Austen's recommendations for a kinder, gentler plantocracy, however, do anything but confront that institution head on. Not to put too fine a point on it, the opposite is virtually true. En route to the new dispensation, Sir Thomas's change of heart is accompanied and contradicted by his challenge to the heterogeneous utterances of those who flout his power. Hence his moral reformation paradoxically reconfirms his control. With unruly elements purged or contained and his unitary discourse intact though

refashioned, the same power relationships persist in slightly different guise between the ruling-class elite and dominated people,
between male and female. Thus to read *Mansfield Park* as a text
with closures that favor more benevolent sociopolitical relationships only serves to mask textual undercurrents that threaten to
explode its tightly controlled bourgeois framework.

Let me briefly recite some of the closures that purport to foretell
future felicity and a more uniform culture groping toward harmony.
First, *Lovers' Vows* is intended to demonstrate how well the Baron
(Sir Thomas) suppresses anarchic expression and restores peace
after learning his lesson. Second, despite announcing her right to
autonomy, protagonist Fanny Price attains the status of an insider
because she mirrors Sir Thomas's values and rather coldly rejects
her origins. She embraces an imposed identity as a bona fide member of the Mansfield Park community. Sir Thomas in turn offers
himself as a father: "Fanny was indeed the daughter that he wanted.
His charitable kindness had been rearing a prime comfort for himself."[53] Third, the Price family in Portsmouth is exposed as decisively inferior except for those who agreeably adapt. Disobedience
and heady self-determination are penalized by lifetime expulsion
from the old order: Maria Bertram and Mary Crawford are excluded
from the ruling-class coterie while younger daughter Julia's repen-
tance and her more accommodating disposition gain her a second
chance.

Also to the point is Lady Bertram's languid life, which is criticized yet accepted as a familiar, though inconsequential, existence
while the mettlesome spirit of the Price survivors goes unapplauded.
In other words, although Lady Bertram may draw sympathetic
attention as a witless figure, the necessity for a social appendage in
female form to round out plantocratic control is never gainsaid. But
perhaps the most morally ambiguous textual judgment concerns
Mrs. Norris herself, whose downfall is treated as her just desserts.
Former overseer and exposed renegade, she is banished for good
from the family circle, like her sister Frances. That she encourages
Maria Bertram to claim a certain kind of freedom is sweepingly

condemned. The text obliterates the fact that she represents Sir Thomas's interests, but in excess of how the text wants him portrayed.[54] She is his avatar, Sir Thomas at his most acquisitive and self-indulgent. He cannot countenance the reflection of himself in Mrs. Norris, who represents his displaced tacit approval of heinous cruelties and ensuing reduced profits. When he rejects her he rejects part of his former self and life; he becomes part of the new order that seeks more wholesome relations at home and abroad. Since his regeneration cannot mean that he continues to treat people unfeelingly, Mrs. Norris has to be reconstructed as a villain, tidily demolished, and eliminated as a speaking subject.

However, in their blanket effort to smother opposition, these methodical but artificial closures only highlight ideological antagonisms that destabilize Sir Thomas's power and question its validity. They elicit an insistent counterdiscourse. His posture also underwrites a certain anxiety about outsiders, regardless of former familial or friendly relationships. Human connections count for naught compared to the obsession with control.

Most ironically, textual embeddings surface in the person of Sir Thomas's major vindicator, the Baron, who turns out in one sense to be his most damning accuser. As Sir Thomas's autocratic counterpart, the medieval Baron has no compunction about killing an innocent man who defies his authority. Similarly, Sir Thomas himself can order severe punishment, although not death, for slaves he arbitrarily deems insubordinate. Such was the authority of planters. And not uncoincidentally, the Baron is execrating Frederick in *Lovers' Vows* while that other Baron, Sir Thomas, administers the Antiguan plantations, by implication in the same way. The Baron denies Frederick's humanity as planters deny the humanity of slaves, relenting only when he discovers Frederick is his son. In a remarkably unconscious self-projection, the Baron commands Frederick in words that would make more sense in reverse: "Desist—barbarian, savage, stop!!"[55] Moreover, by summarily terminating the theatricals, Sir Thomas reestablishes his authority over a symbolically uncontrollable situation.[56]

Mansfield Park: *Plantocratic Paradigms*

Most materially the sparse counterdiscourse concerning slaves pinpoints a fundamental textual repression. Having affirmed her pleasure in Sir Thomas's stories of his Caribbean visit, Fanny inquires about the slave trade. After absorbing her uncle's answer— significantly unreported—she expresses amazement to Edmund about the ensuing "dead silence," a phrase that requires careful unpacking.[57]

In this transitional post-abolitionist period, which features a shaky British-Caribbean economy and multiple slave insurrections, from a Eurocentric perspective no safe space is available for colonized others as speaking subjects, let alone as self-determining agents. Put baldly, slave subjectivity has to be effaced. As the oppressed daughter of an exigent family, Fanny Price becomes the appropriate mediator or representative of slaves' silenced existence and constant insurrectionary potential. In her role as a marginalized other (though in a vastly different cultural context), Fanny Price can project and displace personal-political anxieties and mimic her position as a servile subject position.

As a brief for gradual plantocratic reform, the text disintegrates at "dead silence," a phrase that ironically speaks important debarred and smothered voices. As Mansfield Park's unofficial spokesman for Antiguan society, the beleaguered Sir Thomas has cut slaves off from representation. Besides, *Lovers' Vows* has already voiced and even accentuated the major topoi of a muzzled colonialist discourse: brutality, fractured families, and the violated bodies and psyches of innocent people. Thus the conceptualizations of *dead* and *silence*, which parallel the play's metonyms of bondage, further indict the gaps in Sir Thomas's discourse. Beyond that these loaded inscriptions of death and muteness accost the taboo enforced on dissent in the colonies. "Dead silence" affirms Sir Thomas's seeming pretense that power relations are stable in Antigua. For what, other than dissimulation of some sort—most likely an obfuscation or omission—could explain Fanny Price's ready acceptance of his lengthy speech on the slave trade? *Dead* and *silence*, in other words, forswear the reality of ubiquitous slave insurrections. For example, plots were organized and carried out in Jamaica, Tobago, and especially in Dominica, where the Second Maroon War was led by Quashie, Apollo, Jacko, and others.[58]

Uncontainable conflicts are further unmasked by textual allusions to several issues of the *Quarterly Review*, which carried many troublesome facts about slavery in 1811:[59] For one, the periodical reported that the progressive diminution in slave population levels persisted, despite abolition of the trade, a fact that threw doubt on promises made by planters and colonial legislatures to ameliorate conditions. Old planters in Jamaica and Antigua were in the news, too, as zealous competitors of the "new" planters. The *Quarterly Review* also confirmed that the bottom had dropped out of the sugar market by 1808, that estates were in disrepair, and growers could not be indemnified.[60] What's more, the seemingly univocal colonial discourse of *Mansfield Park*, which upholds a singular view of slavery as "working," belies domestic agitation inside and outside Parliament for improved conditions.[61]

Antigua, then, is a trope for an anxiety-creating unknown venue, falsely coded as a run-down locale in need of an individual planter's semialtruistic, definitively ethnocentric intervention. Profits are down, but workers and administrators suffer, too. Antigua also correlates with Portsmouth, both being symbolic sites of indeterminancy near water and places where the allegedly uncivilized cluster. As a port and an island intimately involved with slavery, Portsmouth and Antigua witness slave ships arriving and departing; scenes involving the sale of people and naval engagements are in constant view. Sir Thomas may subsume Antigua within his monocular vision, and Fanny Price may fail to see (or evade) Portsmouth's obvious immersion in the slave trade as she gazes at the sights of the town, but their buried knowledge and realities circulate intertextually nonetheless. Like the Orient in Edward Said's formulation, Antigua and Portsmouth are Mansfield Park's wild, colonized others, signs of potential disruption and sexual conflict.[62] They mark that the women of Mansfield Park are ideologically absorbed or unceremoniously expelled—or even obliterated (as the slave women of Antigua are) as autonomous beings.

In this space as Mansfield Park's other, Antigua satirizes Sir Thomas's authority. He may conduct his relationships in a recognizably plantocratic mode that solidifies his power, but both vocal and mute suppressions are evident. Sir Thomas's return assumes that he leaves behind a certain order, even harmony, on his plantations. He controls superficially obedient slaves, but that illusion will soon be fractured. By implication other apparent fixtures might also turn out to be less enduring.

This is not to argue that race and gender relations are inextricably linked, that the possibility of slave emancipation in *Mansfield Park* parallels a potential liberation for white British women. But it is to posit that challenges to ossified thought and the received cultural representation of women are at least conceivable. Lady Bertram is comatose, but can that state last? The condition of indolent plantocratic wives is certainly coming to an end. Besides, the self-determining duo of Maria-Mary will not tolerate permanent disappearance. Their independent natures will soon reassert themselves, the text having forced them into a closure, demonstrably false. Fanny Price, however, the obedient daughter who replaces the ungovernable overseer, is pinioned in a conflict of searing and unresolvable tensions. She may have much in common even with the Hart sisters but the text brackets off the conditions of possibility for exercising more freedom. Fanny Price and the Hart sisters, for example, represent the internalization of the prescriptions and individual conscience of evangelical religion. All three are deeply concerned with education. There is also a strong suggestion in all three cases that in this new time aborning, education and internalized religion may at least partially substitute for status and money. So little room is available for repudiation of Fanny Price's place in Mansfield Park's social situation that it threatens to bind and fix her.[63] Ultimately the rebellious acts of Fanny Price and her ideological companions, Maria, Frances Price, and Frederick, are paradigmatic of slave resistance: Fanny Price signifies a bartered slave and the sign of the absent female slave. The deported Maria, in turn, is a variant of the marginalized Portsmouth family.

By contrast Sir Thomas's authority is scarcely denied by the men of the text, who fare somewhat differently. Each projects a part of that complex Sir Thomas, even the sybaritic Bishop Grant, symbolically linked to his malignant niece and nephew, Mary and Henry Crawford, as Sir Thomas is linked to Mrs. Norris. Despite debauchery, elder son Tom will take up his inheritance, as does the foolish Rushworth, whose wealth and aristocratic status enable him to transcend a temporary setback. Henry Crawford continues to seduce women, and Edmund settles down into married life.

Mansfield Park, then, I am arguing, is a post-abolition narrative that intertwines with a critique, conscious or unconscious, of gender relations. Although the text superficially presents itself at the end as an agreeable synthesis that has incorporated its contradictions—the hermeneutics of an attempted restoration of power—the text's relationship to emancipationist ideology creates irrepressible contradictions and flags incompletion. As a colonialist script it features epistemological ethnocentrisms, blanks, ellipses, substitutions, and the homogenizing of silent slaves, occupying a space between old and new modes of discourse and agitation. It projects the end of an uncompromising proslavery lobby by fusing commentary on slaves and Anglo-Saxon women who are concurrently exhibiting forms of autonomy and powerlessness. Thus the reformed planter's voice in itself becomes a nullified force. His contradictory positions cancel themselves out. The indirectness of the commentary, moreover, indicates Jane Austen's temporary reluctance to sound the controversy over slavery into recognizable audibility. Not until *Emma* does she do so unmistakably.

As a quasi-allegory of colonial-gender relations, *Mansfield Park* offers itself as a blueprint for a new society of manners. Relationships in the colonies will match those at home, for domestic manners have been transformed for the better. But as we have seen, Sir Thomas's brand of Eurocentric benevolence is dubious at best, and the sociopolitical recommendations are decidedly and perhaps necessarily constrained. Nonetheless, the attempt to show the positive consequences of a more harmonious world in action, together with many potent silences and eruptions of nuanced subaltern voices, signifies the desirable, though possibly not attainable, transition to a new colonialist dispensation of gradualist politics at home and abroad. Despite this slow but positive evolution, however, emancipation still cannot be named.

Together Mary Wollstonecraft and Jane Austen display the concerns of white women adjusting to a law prohibiting abolition that inevitably precipitates a struggle for emancipation. Their texts, that is, are produced in and because of a historically tempestuous epoch.

In the texts written by Anne Hart Gilbert and Elizabeth Hart Thwaites, black Antiguan female contemporaries of Jane Austen— women that a nonfictional Sir Thomas Bertram might well have known about or met—the vantage point shifts qualitatively. Much more than Mary Wollstonecraft and Jane Austen, Anne and Elizabeth Hart realize how extensively their society constructs them within its dominative hierarchy. Moreover, their response to the condition of slaves and to their environment more generally sheds further light on the narrowness and limitations of Wollstonecraft's and Austen's viewpoints. Perhaps more to the point, the summoning of Elizabeth Hart Thwaites before the Antiguan Privy Council in 1831 to defend her activities suggests that colonial hierarchical relations do not change perceptibly. If anything, the colonial order becomes more insecure and aggressive as emancipation ineluctably approaches.

Sending the Younger
Son Across the Wide
Sargasso Sea:
The New Colonizer Arrives

> I do not like what I have seen of this honour-
> able gentleman. Stiff. Hard as a board and
> stupid as a foot, in my opinion, except where
> his own interests are concerned.
> —Jean Rhys,
> *Wide Sargasso Sea*, pp. 114–15

Wide Sargasso Sea affirms the idea that the colonial order was well advised to feel less secure as emancipation approached. And only disguised aggression, not overt violent aggression, worked as a temporary antidote, as the understated opening avows: "They say when trouble comes close ranks, and so the white people did." Set to the south of Antigua in Dominica, *Wide Sargasso Sea* extends the East Caribbean discussions to another British West Indian island. Written by Jean Rhys, a Dominican from the small white upper class, *Wide Sargasso Sea* (1966) narrates the post-emancipationist subversion by Jamaican and Dominican communities of gender and colonial relations.[1] Set in Jamaica, Dominica, and England in the 1830s, it explores that fluid historical era when black and white communities were adjusting to emancipation. Many-layered, *Wide Sargasso Sea* also comments obliquely on post-emancipation race relations in Jean Rhys's own period with the eruption of the Notting Hill Riots in London in 1958.[2] In that sense Jean Rhys directly and indirectly challenges two worlds of postcolonial emancipation. Although the novel overtly represents renegotiated colonial relations between the colonizer and the freed but still colonized, the text covertly intimates that the African-Caribbean communities drove out the English and the white creoles. In other words, freed slaves reject the new economic order of society based on capital accumulation by residual ex-plantocrats and their patriarchal allies.

Let me briefly recapitulate significant points. Jean Rhys is reconstructing *Jane Eyre* from the point of view of Antoinette, later Bertha Cosway Mason Rochester (part 1), then from the point of view of her husband, Edward Rochester (part 2), and last from the perspective of both Antoinette and Grace Poole, her keeper after Rochester has locked Antoinette in an attic on his English estate.[3] (For convenience I refer to the multiply named female protagonist as Antoinette.) Part 1 concerns Antoinette's childhood and marriage at the Coulibri estate near Spanish Town, Jamaica; her special relationships with African-Caribbean friend Tia and housekeeper Christophine; her mother Annette's marriage to Richard Mason after the post-emancipation death of Antoinette's father, Mr. Cosway; the burning of Coulibri by freed slaves; and Annette Cosway Mason's psychic disintegration. Part 1 also intertextualizes some of Jean Rhys's experiences growing up, especially in Antoinette's awkward and eventually estranged relationship with her mother, her ambiguous, often ethnocentric descriptions of African-Caribbeans, and her eventual withdrawal and keen sense of alienation: "She was white but not English or European, West Indian but not black."[4] Part 2 narrates the honeymoon of Antoinette and Rochester in Granbois, Dominica, their interactions with the servants Amélie and Christophine as well as with Daniel Cosway, who controversially claims to be the son by a black woman of Antoinette's father. Part 3 sketches Antoinette's imprisonment in the attic of Rochester's English "Great House," her torching of that house, and her fatal jump. In contrast to this narrative of complex British-Caribbean interrelationships, Charlotte Brontë's text nearly silences Bertha Rochester—never naming her—and comments only briefly on Rochester's marriage to this white creole heiress. Put differently, it seems unlikely that Brontë could see Bertha at all except as the dangerous sign of Rochester's problematic youth. Rochester is traditionally configured as a tragic hero, victim of a trick marriage.

Precipitating the focal action in *Wide Sargasso Sea* are the Rochesters, a well-connected British family, contemptuous of a meretricious plantocracy but not above exploiting its vulnerable heiresses. (I call the family the Rochesters and the protagonist Edward Rochester, following Jean Rhys's notes for the novel and her transparent reinterpretation of *Jane Eyre*.) Capitalizing on their status, male family members are bent on usurping and administering estates and fortunes, if not restoring the political power of a vanquished and vanishing pre-emancipation planter class.

Duty bound to the law of the father, younger son Edward Rochester journeys to Spanish Town as a potential speculator in order to expropriate through marriage the inheritance of an unknown woman. In Kenneth Ramchand's words, Jean Rhys "is building upon a type situation in island history—the marrying of Creole heiresses for their dowry by indigent, but socially well-connected younger sons."[5]

This updated form of Caribbean predation had become common in the years following the passage of the Emancipation Bill in 1834 and is inscribed in the actions of Edward Rochester's predecessor, his economic forefather of sorts, the heiress's stepfather Mr. Mason. The community observes these white goings-on. A cynical black wedding guest sneers that Rochester came to "make money cheap as they all do. Some of the big estates are going cheap, and one unfortunate's loss is always a clever man's gain" (p. 30). With the encouragement of unscrupulous Richard Mason, stepbrother of his bride-to-be, Rochester has successfully drawn heiress Antoinette Cosway Mason into an economy that only can purport to be a market economy, given the precarious oppositions between freed slaves and former slaveowners within Jamaican and Dominican culture.

In a mental letter to his father, Edward acknowledges his role as an obedient son. He accedes to coercion but cannot entirely stifle his opposition, let alone his suppressed desires:

Dear Father.
The thirty thousand pounds have been paid to me without question or condition. No provision made for her (that must be seen to). I have a modest competence now. I will never be a disgrace to you or to my dear brother the son you love. No begging letters, no mean requests. None of the furtive shabby manoeuvers of a younger son. I have sold my soul or you have sold it, and after all is it such a bad bargain? The girl is thought to be beautiful, she is beautiful. And yet . . .   (p. 70)

Less savory aspects of the transaction, absent in these ruminations, are supplied later in a conversation, which Antoinette overhears, between Richard Mason and her Aunt Cora, ironically a former slaveowner:

"It's disgraceful," she said. "It's shameful. You are handing over everything the child owns to a perfect stranger [Edward Rochester]. Your father would never have allowed it. She should be protected, legally. A settlement can be arranged and it should be arranged. That was his intention."
     . . . He told her for God's sake shut up you old fool and banged the door when he left. So angry that he did not notice

me [Antoinette] standing in the passage. She was sitting up in bed when I went into her room. "Halfwit that the boy is, or pretends to be. I do not like what I have seen of this honourable gentleman. Stiff. Hard as a board and stupid as a foot, in my opinion, except where his own interests are concerned."

(pp. 114–15)

As an investor in women, Edward Rochester can think only in commercial terms that highlight his privileged Anglo-Saxon heritage; he cannot face, he even reverses, the implications of his own acts: "I have not bought her. She has bought me, or so she thinks" (p. 70). He thinks he hears a debased French patois when he hears a complex creole language. What he interprets as inexplicable "blanks in my mind" (p. 76) signify his ignorance, his immersion in the ethic of an imperial country, a steadfast denial of historical facts.

Antoinette is the site of negotiations of power between Rochester and Mason, foreclosing structures protested by herself and Aunt Cora. To her stepbrother she is dispensable property that can be bartered for a respectable lineage, something resident plantocrats rarely possessed but always craved. She is the site of a different version of slavery: A legally free woman is bought because she owns property. A handy commodity, she affords Edward Rochester's father an opportunity to get the younger son rich quick.[6] Male traders at the wedding are mute about the wedding's raison d'être though the groom discloses a sense of his function in an unself-conscious act of displacement when he speaks wryly of planters: "I remember little of the actual ceremony. Marble memorial tables on the walls commemorating the virtues of the last generation of planters. All benevolent. All slave-owners. All resting in peace" (p. 77).

Since Victorian proprieties demand that he stay a seemly amount of time to lend an air of respectability to the marriage, the ill-fitted pair travel with an African-Caribbean retinue to the bride's mother's small estate in Dominica. Yet Daniel Cosway interrupts their honeymoon with allegations about Antoinette's mad family and his own familial connections; discord implodes, then explodes, and never ceases: "I am your wife's brother by another lady, half-way house as we say. . . . They are white, I am coloured. They are rich, I am poor" (pp. 96–97).

In Dominica, Rochester's objectification of Antoinette as a marketable item is matched by his general attitude toward the black population. His insecurities are expressed in anxious body language, obvious to everyone but his unseeing self. "Sometimes a sidelong look or a sly knowing glance disturbed me" (p. 90), he confesses, with no cognizance of his own provocation, the bait of his very presence. He conducts himself as a latter-day Robinson Crusoe, forcibly shipwrecked at his family's instigation among diverse inferiors.[7] Even one of the songs the couple share features a character named Robin, evoking Crusoe-Rochester's imperial encounter, his quest for empire, his preternatural solitude—colonial beginnings that turn out catastrophically for Edward Rochester.

Fearful of losing control and oblivious to his pernicious and multiple interpellations vis-à-vis freed slaves and his newly acquired wife and family network, Rochester's only outlet is self-communion about felt hostility. He never acknowledges that he is married to the daughter of a former slave-owning family, even when he sarcastically notes her casual beneficence toward black servants. To permit any circulation of this history would amount to complicity in institutionalized colonialism. Ironically, of course—or is it symbolically?—his actions echo his father's and are scarcely distinguishable from traditional plantocratic conduct like Old Man Cosway's. Small wonder that Rochester ends up longing for the night and sex since his only formulated plan, as he states in the opening lines of the novel, is to advance and retreat. Awaiting the right moment to retreat without losing face, he marks time while taking full advantage of his new status as husband.

When Daniel Cosway's letter disrupts their nightly sexual stupors, Rochester seizes upon it as the perfect excuse to sail away even more hastily than he had planned. The mirroring of his palpable greed in Cosway's own opportunistic ploy is quite beyond

Rochester's perception. For Daniel Cosway has confirmed Rochester's most overt fears: He has married into a miscegenous family, his white colonial vision is a fraud, the source of his ill-gotten affluence is tainted. Consequently the fact that he feels an uneasy attraction for the island and its way of life, as well as for his wife, somewhat unnerves him and wrestles his horror at Cosway's apparent revelations. He cannot think straight. (Even at the end, after he has abandoned the Caribbean for Britain and joined the absentee landlord class, aping old planters and betraying total alienation, he imagines that he is emotionally proffering Antoinette one last chance. Or he tells himself that he does. Colonial narcissism dictates that she should read his mind. Overseer Baptiste is left in Rochester's place at Granbois after Rochester's humiliating exodus.)

But a nagging question erupts here. Why does Jean Rhys choose the moment when Rochester is surrounded by black islanders—historically constituted as overground maroons—to kill off his father and brother? Is it simply a need of the plot to have Edward Rochester rich in his own right or does it presage his own future fall?

Contextualizing Daniel Cosway's letter explicates Rochester's dread of an oppositional environment. After 1834, when slaves were legally free, planter suicides were not uncommon. Legal compensation they received often had to be paid to insistent creditors, and sugar prices rocketed.[8] By 1847, 140 sugar estates had been abandoned, several of them "miserable worthless places thrown up in consequence of being plunged in debt long before the abolition of slavery."[9] Estate values collapsed:

> 64 petitions of insolvency have been filed; estate after estate thrown upon the market, and no purchaser found. Even where there has been no insolvency, many estates have been abandoned from the inability to raise money on the faith of the coming crop . . . Within the last few weeks Jordan Hill estate

. . . with a crop of 450 to 500 hogsheads on the ground, and on which about £1,500 were expended last year, in laying down tram roads . . . has been sold for £4,000. This sale has taken place, not under an insolvency or bankruptcy, nor to meet the pressure of creditors, but by persons of wealth and respectability; and men here wonder, not at the sacrifice of the vendors so much as the rashness of the purchaser.[10]

Thomas McCormack, a well-known Jamaica estate owner for forty years, "cut his own throat in December 1848 after a period of severe mental depression and immediately following the destruction of his megass house at Stanton by the work of an incendiary. A year earlier sixteen Jamaica planters who owned nineteen estates free of debt or encumbrance and leased another thirteen declared themselves unable to cultivate for another year and incapable, without credit, of taking off the existing crop."[11]

Furthermore, estate owners in Dominica like Rochester fared even worse, another reason why Daniel Cosway's exposé bedevils Rochester. The number of actual Caribbean-based plantation owners diminished to virtual invisibility. As contemporary John Davy states, "In a recent communication from thence, it is stated that the number of resident proprietors (worthy of the name) does not exceed two."[12] Being outnumbered by angry slaves or freed individuals was a colonizer's nightmare.

Other estate owners were absentee landlords. Davy continues: "Of the other class,—the white inhabitants and the planters, I can give but little information, having, though twice in the island, but only a few hours, had no opportunity to become acquainted with them. Of the proprietors of estates, most of the English are, I believe, absentees" (p. 504). Demoralization among despised white property owners in Dominica makes Rochester's near paranoia and sociocultural paralysis a standard reaction for his class:

Neither in the official reports on the state of the island, or in conversation with those connected with it, have I been able to find any proof of advancing intelligent exertion similar to that

97

witnessed in Barbados, Antigua, and St. Kitt's. No attempt that I have heard of has been made to form an agricultural society, or to establish a library, or, in brief, to accomplish anything tending to promote the advancement of knowledge, the acquisition of science, without which, how is it possible at the present time that any people can be successful, even as regards the lowest, their worldly and material interests! I may perhaps, in making these statements, appear to those acquainted with the island, to express myself too strongly, inasmuch as an effort has been made within the last few years to institute in the town of Roseau, a higher school than the ordinary ones, an academy or grammar school, intended for the education of the children of the upper class; but even this, though aided by a proportionally large annual grant of money from the island treasury, does not appear to have been successful, and has been considered by those who ought to be competent judges, the Lieut. Governor and Governor General, as ill-timed and injudicious.[13]

Burnt estates became familiar signifiers of historical resistance and revenge, of a celebratory, post-emancipation landscape. "Certainly," muses Edward Rochester, "many of the old estate houses were burned. You saw ruins all over the place" (p. 133). In point of fact Jamaica and Dominica, the only Caribbean locales named, had mounted severe, unprecedented opposition to the white plantocracy.

Constantly shifting colonial relations made for a traumatized childhood for Antoinette Cosway. They also evoke experiences Jean Rhys shares with Antoinette that further complicate the text. Antoinette grew up lonely and increasingly introspective—a double outsider—able to do little else than internalize the opprobrium of formerly colonized people on whose company and friendship she depended.[14] But realistically, as she sadly confesses, her childhood friend Tia and others "hated us. They called us white cockroaches . . . Nobody wants you" (p. 23).[15] At other times whites were disparaged as centipedes who had to be eliminated. One black witness to the fire on the Coulibri estate explains the need to demolish their presence this way: "You mash centipede, mash it, leave one little piece and it grow again" (p. 43). The population is acutely aware of imperial bonds and continuities. The *glacis* that Annette Cosway paces provides another negative plantocratic association: "The *glacis*, we know, was the wide stone platform for drying coffee. On Sundays and holidays it was here that the slaves would gather to play music and dance."[16] At one level the name of the home itself, *Coulibri*, quietly rebukes its plantocratic linkage. The word derives from a Dominican word—*cou*—for the Great House of the white plantation owner, mellifluously and ironically it is yoked to a version of *libre*, the French adjective for free. On the other hand, most Dominicans would have heard in *Coulibri* a variant of *Colibri*, the standard Carib loan-word meaning humming-bird.

By the time Edward Rochester appears, Antoinette has become so immune to her status as victim that she acquiesces to the marriage after one bold but short-lived refusal pressed by Aunt Cora. On their honeymoon Antoinette almost joyously acknowledges his power over her. After he has trampled the wedding wreath of frangipani, one of the multiple metonyms for the island's cryptic beauty, which eludes and confuses him, she somewhat coyly declares: "You look like a king, an emperor. . . . She knelt near me [continues Rochester] and wiped my face with her handkerchief" (pp. 73–74).

Antoinette has embraced one of the few spaces a powerless woman can occupy—that of the sexually desirable female—now that she has married and thereby relinquished her inheritance. Although she ostensibly is not forced, in this one respect her short, ardently sexual relationship to the "master" resembles a familiar aspect of the relationships many female slaves endured with white owners.

But this union, tenuous at best, needs very little to fracture it, at least from Rochester's point of view. The accusatory letter he receives from Daniel Cosway, claiming he is Antoinette's stepbrother, does the trick. This stranger's claim to kinship means Rochester not only married into a family in which mother Annette and son Pierre are mentally unstable but also has (to his chagrin) married into a family of color. When his anger bursts, he experiences the historical complicity that he has vehemently suppressed. In that sense Cosway's exposé enables Rochester's self-confrontation.

At this point Rhys invites the reader (who is assumed to be white) to sympathize with Antoinette, her chance of a happy life disastrously thwarted once again. After the plural indignities already perpetrated on this naïve planter's daughter, Daniel Cosway's letter is the last straw. (Antoinette's status as a planter's daughter is metonymically linked to the painting of "The Miller's Daughter" on the wall at Coulibri that is destroyed in the fire. She is first framed and objectified, then burned unrecognizably in the final fire.) She is, after all, a white creole who sometimes empathizes with ex-slaves. Unlike unreconstructed Rochester, Antoinette nurtures a form of post-emancipationist self-knowledge: "No more slavery," she says at one point. "Why should *anybody* work? This never saddened me [that the Coulibri estate went wild]. I did not remember the place when it was prosperous" (p. 19). Elicited empathy for Antoinette as victim aside, the text also rationalizes her classic plantocratic attitudes that wrestle her assimilative desires. In two minor, seemingly unrelated incidents Antoinette's apparent conflict betrays some of Rhys's personal conflicts regarding white creole ideology. In the first instance an enraged Antoinette decries childhood friend Tia as a "cheating nigger," an outburst excused on the grounds of fatigue. More important, Rhys suggests that Antoinette's family bears a dual responsibility: they violate her emotional boundaries so cavalierly that she vents understandable anger on her young friend.

The next instance involves an exchange between Antoinette and the major African-Caribbean character in the text, Christophine, Antoinette's nurse and confidante. Antoinette finds Christophine waiting for her after she visits her troubled mother Annette: " 'What you want to go up there for?' " [Christophine] said, and I said, " 'You shut up devil, damned black devil from Hell' " (pp. 134–35).[17]

Antoinette's desire for close friendship with Tia and Christophine, then, has to be juxtaposed against prejudicial remarks that pop out when Antoinette feels frustrated or agonized. Her status as a victimized creole, the silent argument seems to be, permits such indulgence. Its justice never becomes an issue for herself or other whites. Her conflicts, it almost seems, are supposed to speak for themselves and win sympathy. She shares a history with African-Dominicans, and she wants to be one of them but they reject her. Antoinette's largesse toward indigent blacks, scathingly disparaged by Rochester, her beautiful attire imported from the "Paris of the West Indies," while troped as evidence of a new self-respect, specify the indelible, colonizing mentality of a family that has extorted and appropriated Caribbean land, money, and labor over centuries.

Even her munificence is hollower than she realizes because, although Rochester bides his time and meditates about the time being "not yet" (meaning it is not yet time to control her), her money now legally belongs to him. Also unbeknown to naïve Antoinette, the community pockets the "cockroach's" [Antoinette's] handouts with derision. And how could they not; she reaps what her family has sown, her inheritance of their attitudes in mediated form quite transparent. However, it is also true that her mother, Annette Cosway, chides second husband Richard Mason for his distorted views of black Antiguans and for racist language. By transversing such complex attitudes, Rhys disallows an easy decoding of Antoinette as an unreconstructed planter's daughter. Polyphony abounds as nuanced subtexts sidle into the overt text, author and characters at odds with each other.

Antoinette belongs to no one and belongs nowhere. Her self-alienation is unremitting, her subject position such that she can only grasp self-satisfaction moment by moment. A despised, unwilling wife, she feels a commonality with others whom Rochester directly and indirectly dominates. A victim of historical circumstance, she exists in the margins of everyone else's lives. Her dreams betray inner conflicts, mental debate about what lives she can and should live, their enactment an unconscious parody of Christophine's spiritual practices. Mostly they foretell Rochester's imminent menacing, his design to subsume her. But Antoinette never surrenders. She hails, after all, from stock that had hung on to the bitter end in slave colonies and had emancipation thrust upon them. In the last dream she means to rout him singlehand-edly, though it ends up as a pyrrhic victory for both. At her most dehumanized, incarcerated in perpetuity, she finally defines herself by leaping decisively toward Tia and life-in-death. She bridges the wide sargasso sea in an effort at black-white union and positive connection.

Wide Sargasso Sea, then, represents a struggle between old and new colonial enemies who act defensively toward African-Caribbeans and each other. Antoinette envies others' lives and feels excluded and by turns forlorn or arrogant; Rochester discerns that his wife, as well as the community, has rejected him and fluctuates between an aggrieved self-importance and desire for revenge. The couple negotiate their marital relationship almost as if the old colonizer awaits reconstitution by the heir apparent. In Rhys's formulation the old and now effete plantocracy is appropriately feminized while its usurpers are properly male. In the meantime the always aware and formerly colonized are bent on self-determination and exercis-ing diverse psychological pressure on Edward Rochester and his wife, the daughter of a white plantation owner during slavery.

Daniel Cosway, the black servant Amélie, and Christophine—to take salient examples—mount mordant attacks on Rochester, whose Eurocentricity blinds him to their interconnections. His first move is to transform Daniel Cosway's damning letter, which ex-plains family connections, into an accusation against Antoinette and his general situation; the letter becomes his rationale for enact-ing what his opening words in Dominica purport: to advance into the Caribbean, acquire a fortune, and retreat. Cosway's letter serves to dismantle Rochester's efforts to institute a new postcolonial order that privileges whites; it helps to reconfigure colonial and gender relations by precipitating a struggle to the death between the white pseudo-elite and the black communities. Rochester is forced to face the fact that he cannot construct his environment as he desires; he cannot refashion a pre-emancipation colonial scenario. Daniel Cosway confronts Rochester with ambiguous speculations as well as facts; he resites Rochester's position in the African-Caribbean community. The letter represents as-yet-unspoken versions of events hitherto told univocally by Rochester and Antoinette.

Rochester's Jamaican and Dominican environments now speak out from many sides with many voices and expose mythologies he has been nurturing about unilateral power. His anticipation that nighttime will bring sexual safety turns out to be just as unrealistic as Mr. Mason's false assurances that all will be well the night Coulibri burns to the ground. The new colonial order is so patently out of touch that its members have to be almost physically expelled before they will face facts; material relations have changed fundamentally. This new dispensation longs to live in a past they can control.

Staff members at Granbois, the Dominican estate, and in particular the African-Caribbean women, sabotage Rochester's planned appropriation of Cosway-Mason land and money. They resemble servants at Coulibri like Myra, who overheard and presumably acted upon Mason's talk of "import[ing] coolies . . . from the East Indies" (p. 35). Their tactics range from poison, medicine, and spiritual practices to eavesdropping, games of trickery, withdrawal of labor, psychological maneuvers, and sex.

From the first day of the honeymoon, obeah woman Christophine dissolves any hope Rochester might have cherished for a smooth life.[18] The night they arrive the honeymooners might toast "to our love and the day without end which would be tomorrow," but in that very tomorrow, Rochester discovers he cannot do as he chooses: he wanted to "take her in my arms . . . [and] undo the careful plaits" (p. 84). Instead Christophine serves them breakfast, even though Antoinette informs Rochester that she has sent her servant away twice (p. 84). When he comes out of the bathroom Christophine invites (taunts) him: "Taste my bull's blood, master" (p. 85). She challenges the primacy of his authority, reallocates it to herself. Internally he castigates "their lying talk" as she reprimands him about the mess he has created: "It bring cockroach in the house" (p. 85). Thus Christophine warns him that if he acts typically (like a cockroach, a troublesome nocturnal pest that hides in moist places during the day), he will reap a grim harvest.

Christophine's signifying name should have put Rochester on guard, but his insensitivity to the world around him occluded such insight. Certainly Jean Rhys alerts the reader, through nomenclature, of Christophine's power. A christophine, or *choco,* is a common Caribbean plant with a wholesome, succulent fruit. But its particularly striking feature is its growth of tendrils, which enable the fruit to spread and grow anywhere. A variant name for a christophine fruit is *chayote,* which mimes in reverse phonemes the name of neighboring St. Vincent's maroon revolutionary hero, Joseph Chatoyer. A famous letter found in Joseph Chatoyer's pocket after he was killed in battle by a British Major Leith in St. Vincent in 1795 exhorted: "We do swear that both fire and sword shall be employed against them [the white British], that we are going to burn their estates, and that *we will murder their wives and children,* in order to annihilate their race." [19]

In rage at one point Rochester refers to Christophine as "Josephine," a feminized designation of her revolutionary namesake, Joseph Chatoyer. [20] Raising the issue of power, Josephine is also the first wife of Napoleon and a woman from Martinique. Obviously, too, Christophine's name echoes that of Henri Christophe, first crowned king of independent Haiti. To augment these links with power, Christophine's last name, Dubois (literally translated, "of the wood") intertextualizes the celebrated resistance by maroons (living in rain forests) for which these two islands, Jamaica and Dominica, were especially renowned. As a practitioner of obeah, moreover, *Christophine* is a heavily ironic appellation: The first syllable evokes Christ in the context of a culture in which Christianity overlays and becomes syncretized with African belief systems. Christophine, in a sense, subsumes Rochester and his values and proclaims the power of Caribbean culture. Implicit in Christophine's name is the firm notion of struggle and revolution against colonial domination.

This metaphorical density of Christophine's name makes Rochester's remark, when he strides angrily through the forest, even more telling: "I knew how to avoid every creeper [tendril] and I never stumbled once" (p. 139). Rochester imagines he is above being interfered with or halted in his colonial tracks. He scarcely realizes that the interventions have already occurred, that the end of his life as a colonizer is more or less in sight. As the major representative of freed slaves Christophine can entangle him as no one else can, and shortly after Rochester's sojourn in the woods she proves his fears justified. In public she boldly challenges his abuse of Antoinette. In earshot of witnesses at Granbois, to his fury she harshly intones a litany of his duplicity and greed. A powerful member of the community denounces the political overlord; she exorcises his presence from the community.

At a further metaphorical level Christophine's name constitutes in the book another causeway—a bridge over marshy land—in that her name's link to maroons unpacks Annette Cosway's early lamentation: "Now we are marooned" (p. 18). Antoinette and Rochester later are always marooned—surrounded, that is, by insurgents whose opposition they neither acknowledge nor recognize.

After Christophine has taken Rochester to task for his treatment of Antoinette, he is reduced to a mimic, repeating her words and her questions; he becomes the Coulibri parrot with clipped wings, identified with Antoinette's mother, Annette, that tries hopelessly to identify intruders—Qui est là? Rochester cannot hear himself echoing the original colonial vanguard, a pathetic creature (like Annette) killed in combat. He threatens Christophine: "You'll go or I'll get the men to put you out." Her answer flaunts the fact that the community is, as its name embeds, a unity—people do their jobs, collect their salary, little more: "You think the men here touch me? They not damn fool like you to put their hand on me" (p. 159). Even when it is based on fear of obeah, the solidarity of the ex-slaves supersedes white authority.

Christophine destabilizes Rochester's power and empowers herself before his very eyes and in front of onlookers. She publicly humiliates him. That she is the one community member who manifestly makes a fool of him comes as no surprise, for her disrespect stands in inverse proportion to the treatment she received: she was presented to Antoinette as a wedding gift. In a superbly orchestrated display of poetic justice, an old slave-owning colonizer's gift becomes the prideful denouncer—almost the executioner—of the new colonizer. Revising Hélène Cixous's formulation, Christophine dares to make unheard-of intersections with Rochester, the other; she deracinates invisibility. Now, ironically, she wields more power through obeah practices than does Antoinette, the creole wife: "For once she blazes *her* trail . . . . And for good reason. There will have been the long history of gynocide. This is known by the colonized peoples of yesterday, . . . those who are locked up know better than their jailers the taste of free air. . . . On the one hand she has constituted herself necessarily as that 'person' capable of losing a part of herself without losing her integrity. But secretly, silently, deep down inside, she grows and multiples."[21] Christophine's challenge to white hegemony increases the chance of cultural autonomy. Rochester empowers her by treating her as a dire threat. Attempts to discipline her engender opposite results. By dogging Rochester's actions, goading him into further misadventure, and harassing Antoinette Cosway somewhat more subtly and protractedly, the African-Caribbeans inexorably negotiate their way toward new freedoms. Or to put it slightly differently, Frantz Fanon's analysis of mimicking locates Rochester as someone constructed in another's master discourse; freed slaves have become the masters, and his only recourse is to echo them deferentially. His mimicking constitutes a surrender of power to the other, an ultimate collaboration.[22]

In addition to Daniel Cosway and Christophine, Amélie is a third subaltern who operates as an insurgent double agent. From the start of his honeymoon Rochester is visibly affected by her presence and conventionally encodes her as a vamp-hussy. To devastate Antoinette he seduces Amélie, or so he thinks, but unbeknown to him, the servant has devised a protracted plan to outwit him. His arrogance, perhaps his expectation that women will be available and pliable, causes him to fall for it. As the deliverer of Daniel Cosway's letter, Amélie notes its impact on Rochester and prepares herself. The morning after their sexual encounter, which had been building up because of her calculated flirting, she is ready to leave for her sister's in Rio, her fear of Christophine another key factor. Amélie turns the main trope of the white couple's bonding—sex—against Rochester and Antoinette while respecting the black power-figure. Patiently waiting for the right opportunity while simultaneously mimicking the master's game and ridiculing him, Amélie avenges herself and the community for Antoinette's lineage and for her animosity and ill-concealed jealousy. She exploits Rochester's desire to teach Antoinette a lesson by using her black woman's body to her own end.

The fact that Christophine and Rochester in tandem, but for different reasons, compare and even confuse Antoinette and Amélie underpins personal interconnections that still remain between the community and vestigial white creoles. Rochester conflates them as sexual service stations and suspects miscegenous relationships everywhere. As Rochester states before his fierce argument with Antoinette: "She [Antoinette] raised her eyebrows and the corners of her mouth turned down in a questioning, mocking way. For a moment she looked very much like Amélie. Perhaps they are related, I thought. It's possible, it's even probable in this damned place" (p. 127). In speculating on Amélie's relation to Antoinette, he projects an incestuous desire. His implied guilt at daily indulged sexuality is partly assuaged when he engages with a black woman upon whose body such excesses are traditionally expected and condoned. He is oblivious to the rancor he radiates. The next morning the cook leaves, emblemizing the end of all nurturance.

Christophine, on the other hand, blends the unlikely pair together because she despises any human exploitation; she excoriates Amélie's antics toward Rochester and upbraids Antoinette for slave-owning connections. She wants to uphold standards of behavior for the community while assuming rapacious, self-serving conduct on the part of whites. Amélie is "worthless and good for nothing, she creep and crawl like centipede" (p. 102). On the other hand, when Rochester acts despotically, openly contemptuous of all others, she leaves. At a distance she can be detached and more in control. At this critical juncture opposed ideologies in the text clash. Christophine's departure from Granbois saps Antoinette of confidence. She can cope only as long as she has Christophine to lean on. Consequently, when Rochester baits Antoinette by having intercourse with Amélie within earshot, she heads for Christophine's home in the woods. Antoinette commandeers the narrative, wrests it from Rochester, as it were. Her alliance with Christophine silences the new colonizer, just as Daniel Cosway's letter makes him revert atavistically to the plantocratic ethic. Hence Christophine's strategy effectively causes the couple's separation, metonymic of the routing of white power from the Caribbean.

More happens besides. Not only does Rochester "lose" his narrative at this salient point, but in the course of Christophine's negotiations with Rochester, Antoinette also stops speaking. Mediated through Christophine, the representative of the white creole plantocracy is absorbed (assimilated) by the indigenous people. In the last section, when Rochester almost succeeds in transforming Antoinette into what he desires, a madwoman who will validate a neocolonizer's inhuman actions, African-Caribbeans—not even present—nullify his power over Antoinette. Antoinette conjures up Christophine and Tia as living presences before she leaps into the flames that destroy his property. They inspire her and provoke her victorious yet tragic decision. She dies as she lived, torn between old and new worlds, alienated from both on one hand and uniting them on the other, in an eternal posture of conflict.

In the course of interceding for Antoinette, Christophine reflects her plantocratic double, Aunt Cora; like Cora, Christophine forces Rochester to face his moral bankruptcy. Although he affects not to care if he and Antoinette separate, he cannot stomach the idea of her as another man's property. He may have had marriage forced upon him but personal and family mercenary values, patriarchal and colonial tendencies, ultimately coincide. Whether or not he covets her as a possession, Antoinette must belong to him exclusively. Unwilling to countenance his jealousy, he blames Christophine for the events; in classical reaction formation, he attributes to others his own self-serving aggressive act. He flees with Antoinette to England where she will be treated as his historical misfortune, a crazy wife whom he mercifully incarcerates in his own attic, not an institution; his retinue will pamper him for being a martyr. They will never know that he opted to degrade her in this way rather than manumit her, even symbolically.[23] His moods will not only be forgiven, they will be admired.

Despite multiple interventions from Daniel Cosway, Amélie, and Christophine, Rochester nonetheless still imagines he wields control, oblivious to the final realignment of oppositions against his status as an expropriated landowner. When he assaults Christophine, the most important African-Caribbean in the text and a purveyor of obeah, his only recourse is a plantocratic classic. He threatens her with his civil power, with jail. He reminds her that all whites, more or less, are in complicity. He will have her locked up just as he will lock up Antoinette. He uses the power of patriarchal, colonial institutions that affirm his class to stifle the people's culture and to further tyrannize marginalized African-Caribbean and white women. His collaborator is Mr. Fraser, a friend of the Cosways'. Ironically, his in-laws' legal counsel enables him (he thinks) to get rid of Christophine, the one person who defends

Antoinette and argues for justice. The moral world of the old and new colonizer has become a world turned upside down.

Despite Rochester's efforts to impose a Western scenario on the Caribbean, to treat African-Caribbeans as nonentities and deleted subjects, they never define him as anything besides the other. Rochester may represent the history of a European return, with all implied threats of mastery, but the community, despised objects of his observations, dissolve the rights he assumes to "take up . . . airs of superiority." Orientalizing, they assert, is at least a two-way street. Rochester learns the hard way that African-Caribbeans are representing themselves in an oblique cancelation of the white legal power that formerly controlled them.[24] Exerting constant pressure on the overlord is part of a collective will within subordinated communities to determine the destiny of the island, to nullify his threats of usurpation, to delete *him* as a subject.

Although Rochester remains vocal to the end, his agency has disintegrated. What counts for him is no longer his power but what other people are saying, how they are looking at him: He worries that Baptiste despises him; he notes that Hilda, the cook, has left without bidding him farewell; he parrots back to them admonitions by Daniel Cosway and Christophine. His authority has vaporized. The resistance script he hears all around him drowns out the colonizer's script. Even the gaze of the colonizer is denied him. His ostensible sign of control—the departure for Europe and a bankrupt "civilization"—also bespeaks his alterity; he is forced to retreat. The black community silently controls him, as his wild thoughts betray not only his inability to master the situation but his realization of impotence and the dual independent conspiracies of his family, as well as the island communities, to manipulate him. He is reduced to a fugitive status that necessitates taking an old colonizer—a form of himself—as prisoner. In a sense he becomes the community's ventriloquist, with Antoinette as a secondary dummy who can be voiced when memories of past life revivify her. The combined historical memory of the community and Antoinette undo him.

The African-Caribbean narrative mirrors his duplicities, its surplus meanings, the past and present oppositions it represents, like Christophine's final words, bespeaking the text's powerful unconscious. The stranger Rochester is a known and unfeared quantity:[25]

"You think you fool me? You want her money but you don't want her. It is in your mind to pretend she is mad. I know it. The doctors say what you tell them to say. That man Richard he say what you want him to say—glad and willing too, I know. She will be like her mother. You do that for money? But you wicked like Satan self!"

I said loudly and wildly, "And do you think that I wanted all this? I would give my life to undo it. I would give my eyes never to have seen this abominable place."

She laughed. "And that's the first damn word of truth you speak. You choose what you give, eh? Then you choose. You meddle in something and perhaps you don't know what it is." She began to mutter to herself. Not in patois. I knew the sound of patois now.

She's mad as the other, I thought, and turned to the window.

The servants were standing in a group under the close tree. Baptiste, the boy who helped with the horses and the little girl Hilda.

Christophine was right. They didn't intend to get mixed up in this business.

When I looked at her there was a mask on her face and her eyes were undaunted. She was a fighter, I had to admit. Against my will I repeated, "Do you wish to say good-bye to Antoinette?"

"I give her something to sleep—nothing to hurt her. I don't wake her up to no misery. I leave that for you."

"You can write to her," I said stiffly.

"Read and write I don't know. Other things I know." She walked away without looking back.   (pp. 160–61)

In the end Christophine simultaneously disappears and disperses herself through the rest of the text; Rhys seems unable to choreo-

graph a satisfactory position for the major African-Caribbean protagonist.[26] Perhaps Christophine's personal oppositional consciousness is beyond Rhys's imaginings.[27] The text is at an impasse and
cannot respond to itself.

Nonetheless, despite Christophine's physical absence, the register of subaltern voices resonates. Not only does the community
silently speak through and to Rochester but two of its members
burn into Antoinette's imagination before the blaze. Rhys's choice
of a fire does more than invoke estate burnings. In autobiographical
terms she talks about associations growing up among England, fires,
and deprivation: "I thought a great deal about England, not fac-
tually but what I had read about it. I pictured it in the winter, a
country covered with snow and ice but also with millions upon
millions of fires. Books, especially Dickens's, talked of hunger,
starvation and poverty but very rarely of cold. So I concluded that
either the English didn't feel the cold, which surely wasn't possible,
or that everybody had a fire."[28] The community's unassailable
power dominates despite the white creole author's transparent intention to heroinize the victimized Antoinette. Rochester is pressed
into taking oppression that he transported to the islands back home
to England. He abandons his pseudocolonial fiefdom, a figure of
contempt left with nothing more than an empty symbol—his alienated wife of a trick marriage. The days of richly laden vessels
exporting sugar and coffee to England are gone, and their replace-
ment pitifully reflects the colonial loss of power. Leaving the Caribbean Rochester has written himself out of the human community,
an unwitting, unwilling vindicator of people's justice. The book's
title, *Wide Sargasso Sea*, supplements the text's refusal to accede to
any classic realist closure. The novel is named after a sea that is
chockablock with sargassum seaweed and devoid of the plankton
that supply basic food to fish. The particular type of sargassum that
grows in the Sargasso Sea cannot reproduce sexually but only by
fragmentation.[29] These colonizers, old and new, the title suggests,
cannot reproduce themselves. They can only foster further distorted
self-images.[30]

So the finale—Antoinette's jump to Tia—mocks the opening line and is every bit as elliptical: "They say when trouble comes close ranks, and so the white people did" (p. 17). Divided whites cannot close ranks, but one white can unite with Tia across the wide Sargasso Sea—provided Tia is willing—and start some intercultural bonding. More than that, the Caribbean cannot contain whites any more. They are people too divorced from life-affirming principles and from one another.

The last section, told principally by Grace Poole, Antoinette's keeper in the attic, and Antoinette herself recapitulates the lives of slaves who were locked up in cellars and barns, victims of systematic abuse. The attic of Thornfield Hall, Rochester's estate, provides an analogue to atrocious conditions of existence that continually punctuated the pages of pre-emancipation polemics and periodicals. To push the argument as far as it can go, Antoinette burns down the Great House, not just for atonement but as a representative insurrectionist who refuses the role of Sir Thomas Bertram's mute slaves. She will not be complicitous any longer in the "dead silence" of colonialism. In that sense Antoinette torches the Mansfield Park estate and symbolically avenges the colonized against the plantocratic class—both pre- and post-emancipation.[31]

Though immobilized, Antoinette strikes back with her only remaining weapon—a vivid memory. No matter how Rochester tries to deaden her with a protracted, bestial existence, she sporadically creates herself anew, resurrects parts of her old self. Like slaves of old she attempts to murder the owner of the Great House. Moreover and just as much to the point, instead of fleeing or resisting as many slaves did, she opts for that other time-honored alternative, long considered one of the quintessential revolutionary acts of slavery—suicide. Perhaps as a sign of identification, she wants to enter Jamaican-Dominican mythology. Any way she can, Antoinette becomes a different kind of Cosway: she tries to build a link with those earlier allies, Tia and Christophine, and with maroons too, with Rochester's designated others, in short.[32] Her suicide mimics the actions of slaves, of communities she could not join. Clinical or not, her madness derives from the anarchy of colonizers in a last ditch stand. She recognizes Rochester's inhumanity and in doing so, she acknowledges heinous past actions of her family toward slaves. In groping to avenge herself she vindicates the actions of insurrectionary slaves and attempts atonement.

Jean Rhys has recirculated a version of *Jane Eyre* in which she rewrites Charlotte Brontë's story of female identity. She refashions a female literary tradition, destabilizing its paradigmatic consciousness. Rochester is held accountable, and madness is problematized. His decision to lock a woman up for years more than justifies her attack on step-brother Richard Mason when he visits her in the attic and reminds her of her legal status and his original negotiations with Rochester; her "lowering look," attributed by the community to a condition derived from her mad family, is also encoded as a sign at the wedding that she knows what is destined to befall her. Her dreams signify the same way.

The narrative logic of the text upholds the author's planter-descendant politic only if we "believe" the closure of the original text, *Jane Eyre*. In *Wide Sargasso Sea*, instead, Rochester is the Coulibri parrot demanding to know who is there—Qui est là?—fighting him at the end; then he dies with his wings clipped in an act of symbolic justice. Even so, whether African-Caribbeans will celebrate or organize themselves after whites abandon the islands is left as an open question. On that question Jean Rhys also challenges the gender and colonial politics of her own exiled world in Britain.

Before Jean Rhys wrote *Wide Sargasso Sea* in the 1950s, two events occurred that were particularly relevant to her discussion in the novel: First, national, anticolonial independence movements erupted all over the world; second, African-Caribbean people emigrated to Britain in large numbers, a situation that culminated in ugly riots against black people in London and the provinces in 1958.[33] Thus only the suppressed of *Wide Sargasso Sea* hold out the possibility of a macrocosmic victory. Overtly readers witness Antoinette's and Rochester's doubled-edged triumphs: she "wins" because she leaps to Tia and life-in-death but dies anyway.[34] Excluded and unknown, she still terminates his family ties to the islands. He "wins" because, while he is left with her money unencumbered, he is wounded and socially displaced. He lives back home as an insider and outsider, a historical anachronism. If he dies in the fire—an optional reading not excluded in this text—then *Wide Sargasso Sea* is a different story. As it stands the revised text of *Jane Eyre* offers no closure.

At the manifest level, then, the text favors Jean Rhys's class— the former white planter class to which Antoinette belongs. She is meant to be a tragic heroine, and although Rochester is represented as a villain, his family forced him and he was dutiful. Excuses have been concocted since the beginning for his abysmal conduct in locking a woman up *sine die*. At the same time Jean Rhys foregrounds African-Caribbean protagonists and the community as Charlotte Brontë never did. Christophine is a critical hero, although she and other members of the Jamaican and Dominican communities resist being shunted awkwardly out of the text to assert an oppositional agency. From a class, race, and gendered perspective, Jean Rhys cannot allow the implied victors of the text to be articulated as victors. That judgment lies in texts whose vested interest lies elsewhere. One such judgment resides in the texts of black Antiguan writer Jamaica Kincaid. In the past decade Kincaid's novel and polemical essay, *Annie John* and *A Small Place*, respectively, have documented a young woman's complex personal and political reaction to growing up in Antigua and have offered a searing vision of the island by a former resident now living abroad.

A Small Place: *Glossing*
Annie John's Rebellion

Free is how you is from the start, an' when it
look different you got to move, just move, an'
when you movin' say that it is a natural freedom that make you move.

—George Lamming,
quoted in C. L. R. James,
"The Making of the Caribbean People,"
p. 189

In *Annie John* and *A Small Place* Jamaica Kincaid intertwines discussions of gender relations with colonial and postcolonial rebellion.
Annie John (1985) narrates eight stories about Annie John's childhood and burgeoning womanhood from ten to seventeen years of
age on the island of Antigua in the eastern Caribbean, a British
Crown colony at the time.[1] In *A Small Place* (1988) Jamaica Kincaid's political exposé glosses and intertextualizes *Annie John*;[2] it
represents a version of Annie John's "revisionary struggle" as Ja-

maica Kincaid reexamines conflicts that Annie John intimated but could not identify.

Annie John opens on Antigua roughly a year after the first major race riots, precipitated by discrimination against Caribbean immigrants, erupted in London in 1958. In contrast to events at the metropolitan center, Antigua seems peaceful, at least on the surface. Jamaica Kincaid is open about the fact that *Annie John* has a personal dimension and has stated that the feelings in it are autobiographical.[3] Written as a polemic, *A Small Place* betrays no such ambiguity about its autobiographical content.

Both texts extend the discussion of Antigua since Jamaica Kincaid was born Elaine Potter Richardson in St. Johns, Antigua, in 1949. Her father worked as a carpenter and cabinetmaker; her mother was a homemaker and a well-known political activist. At seventeen Elaine Richardson left Antigua for the United States and eventually became a staff writer for the *New Yorker* as Jamaica Kincaid.[4]

Annie John records a maturing girl's experiences growing up in an artisanal family similar to Jamaica Kincaid's, in the midst of the seemingly paradisal world of Antigua. Annie John, however, quirkily obsesses on death. This fascination that Annie John initially expresses marks certain subterranean debates as she struggles with adolescence and colonial reality. In partial response to her rebellious nature and as her mother tries to encourage a more independent existence, Annie John succeeds well in school but refuses to bow to authority. Continually negotiating contradictory positions from the center to the margins and back, sometimes occupying both spots simultaneously, she fuses sexual and cultural innocence with a finely honed bravado and self-justifying duplicities.

Gender Relations

Annie John sublimates feelings of abandonment into conflicted bitterness toward her mother, her dislike magnifying as she mentally augments the gap between them. In her torment she envisions

her mother as a manipulative tyrant, characterizing her as a croco-
dile one moment and in the next as the prey of murderous snakes—
overlapping projections of her frustration. The nurturing of hatred,
a fear of alienation, and a craving to return to intimate bonding
plague her by turn. She secretly harbors a self-conception so mon-
strous that she has induced a desire for separation in her mother;
this negative self-image further indicates that she projects a growing
self-hatred. In another sense Annie John displaces onto her mother
an antagonistic representation of her agonized feelings of rejection
that in turn engender psychic fragmentation. Since her birth she
has lived in her mother's shadow and now that she has to fend for
herself in her own spotlight, as it were, she seeks shade, assuming
she cannot live up to her mother's level of competence; since she
cannot conceptualize her mother's cultural construction, she cease-
lessly tries to fashion a subjectivity in opposition. All of this she
internalizes.

When Annie John reads aloud to her classmates about idyllic
times spent with her mother vacationing on Rat Island as a small
child, she alters the story to hide current mother-daughter disaffection. She confides her pain to the reader: "I placed the old days'
version before my classmates because, I thought, I couldn't bear to
show my mother in a bad light before people who hardly knew her.
But the real truth was that I couldn't bear to have anyone see how
deep in disfavor I was with my mother" (p. 29). Notably, the
paradisal story involves water and simple childhood pleasures as if
she were not only retelling a favorite story but imagining, too, a
return to primal, undifferentiated harmony.[5] In Hélène Cixous's
terms she desires her mother's milk.[6]

Deliberately shunning and depriving herself of a female model,
fixating on her mother as treacherous, she molds herself into an
exciting, desirable subject who obeys and disobeys at will. Her
unconscious battle with social conditioning, an already constructed
subjectivity, explains much of the subsequent tension. In an extensive account of the fight between herself and her mother over
dominance and autonomy, symbolized by marbles, the issue emerges

118

as palpably gender-specific when her mother tells her, "I am so glad you are not one of those girls who like to play marbles" (p. 61). She is trying to create a lady-like daughter. In direct defiance Annie John stays behind after school and arranges to play with the dirty, unruly, nameless Red Girl who punches, then kisses her in an adolescent sexual merry-go-round. She admires the Red Girl's nonconformity and her apparent ability to act as she pleases; she constitutes an alter ego of sorts, certainly a projection of who Annie John would like to be if only to anger her mother.[7] Annie John eventually succeeds in becoming a champion marbles player against express maternal wishes, a thinly veiled metaphor for personal power and successful experimentation.

Annie John secretes her marbles under the bed away from her mother's prying eyes and, by faking homework assignments, she meets clandestinely with the Red Girl. To please herself and trick her mother, she steals money to buy seductive gifts for her friend: "multi-colored grosgrain ribbon or a pair of ring combs studded with rhinestones, or a pair of artificial rosebuds suitable to wear at the waist of a nice dress . . . I simply loved giving her these things . . . it was a pleasure to see they [the parents] didn't know everything" (p. 64).

Playing marbles is a self-directed, symbolic apprenticeship at a time when she already loathes being apprenticed to a seamstress picked out by her mother.[8] Disobeying and abandoning her mother emotionally—a qualified revenge, a victory over surveillance—she becomes an artist in her prowess at marbles and in her appreciation of their appearance. At one level the marbles are embryos of the breasts all her adolescent female friends covet, but they are also beautiful orbs of defiance that proliferate; they have to be concealed, are exchangeable and always desirable. At another level marbles resemble the stolen library books Annie John conceals, treasures that signify rebellion against constraining gender roles, a personal power gained by outwitting authority, and an obsession with knowledge that rivals her previous obsession with death. By stowing books and marbles away she breaks from the adult world and begins to build an alternate way of knowing and doing. Declining to be a gracious object, a lady for the community to admire, or even mother's helper around the house, she constructs herself against the cultural grain through subterfuge. She will not and cannot renounce desire and self-determination.

At other points Annie John edges toward even more overt intimations of subversion, agony, and sexuality. As early as chapter 2, tellingly entitled "The Circling Hand," the twelve-year-old describes her relationship with her parents and their relationship with each other. She recalls old events that wounded her parents: accounts of her mother arguing with her father (Annie John's grandfather), then leaving the childhood home in Dominica, of Annie John's own father waking up in bed with his grandmother dead beside him. Annie John also notes how she once came home from church to discover her parents "lying in their bed" (p. 30). To announce her presence, she aggressively rattles knives and forks, vociferously denying how much this scene affects her. Nevertheless, she obsesses on her mother's hand in a sex- and death-related fantasy that unduly fascinates her; she imagines the hand that caresses her father's back to be that of a skeleton.

These inchoate emotions, stemming from unconscious jealousy, even a buried matricidal wish, explode in a painful remark to her mother as she arranges the cutlery just after the scene. Her mother "looked at me, . . . and walked away. From the back, she looked small and funny. She carried her hands limp at her sides. I was sure I could never let those hands touch me again; I was sure I could never let her kiss me again. All that was finished" (pp. 31–32). Minutes later she disrupts a weekly arrangement. She declines a quiet father-daughter harmony they enjoy on their Sunday walk together: "On our walk, my father tried to hold my hand, but I pulled myself away from him, doing it in such a way that he would think I felt too big for that now" (p. 32). She masks and compensates for her anger and insecurity by designating proximity as her mother's privilege. Parental sexuality bothers the adolescent child; her entry into adolescence and the foreign feelings this generates transform the stirrers of these feelings into "alien parents."[9] The next day she figuratively transfers her overweening maternal love to her friend Gwen, whom she has met at school: "At the end of the day, Gwen and I were in love, and so we walked home arm in arm together. When I got home, my mother greeted me with the customary kiss and inquiries. I told her about my day, going out of my way to provide pleasing details, leaving out, of course, any mention at all of Gwen and my overpowering feelings for her" (p. 33).

Eventually Annie John becomes severely ill. Feeling deprived of maternal care she forgoes all sustenance, akin to stressing self-sufficiency and denial. Yet her refusal affirms her impotence, keeps sexual growth at bay, and attracts hyperattentiveness as she becomes temporarily anorexic.[10] During this prolonged, cryptic illness she experiences unfamiliar sensations after she becomes drenched in bed. As her parents bathe Annie John and change her bed-clothes, her distressed father, dressed in his underwear, holds her in his lap:

> Through the folds of my nightie, I could feel the hair on his legs, and as I moved my legs back and forth against his the hair on his legs made a swoosh, swoosh sound, like a brush being rubbed against wood. A funny feeling went through me that I liked and was frightened of at the same time, and I shuddered. At this, my father, thinking I was cold, hugged me even closer. It dawned on me then that my father, except for when he was sick, slept in no clothes at all, for he would never sleep in clothes he had worn the day before. I do not know why that lodged in my mind, but it did. (pp. 112–13)

Masturbatory fantasy and the involuntary sexual arousal for her father coexist with a regression to infantilism, a reenactment of pre-oedipal immersion in amniotic fluid; water is the primary signifier. By inscribing Annie John's psychic watershed in the title of the chapter, "The Long Rain," Kincaid provides a dense, elemental metaphor to represent the terrifying feelings that threaten to engulf

121

Annie. Illness accentuates her longing for motherly attention. To put the case more forcibly, grief has engendered sickness because she equates separation with annihilation. In the earlier Rat Island episode, when she can no longer discern her swimming mother, "a huge black space then opened up in front of me" (p. 43). Anguish blots out the light, conveying a temporary abdication from life. Thus during her illness she recapitulates a primal scene in which water, womblike, surrounds her and engages the undivided attention not only of her mother but also (unwomblike) of her father. This pre-oedipal merging encompasses a strange form of sexual difference, a means of bonding with both parents, a refusal to allow them as a pair to be separate from her as the one. A bizarre incident symbolically illuminates and further problematizes her inner turmoil. As she lies in bed, family photographs agitate her to such a degree that she feels compelled to wash them, both "the creases in Aunt Mary's veil" and "the dirt from the front of my father's trousers" (p. 120). Meaning slides metonymically from washing to a sexual sign; purity dissolves the possibility of birth.[11] She then lays the saturated photographs to rest in a perfumed bed of talcum powder, a miniature erotic grotto. The performance of this purification-obliteration ritual soaks her nightgown and sheets. She has enveloped herself in a primal reprise, rubbing out faces that speak the life of family members: "None of the people in the [ironic] wedding picture, except for me, had any face left. In the picture of my mother and father, I had erased them from the waist down" (p. 120). Immersion has become self-definition as she metonymically resites herself in the security of the womb. In and with this water she can gain freedom. She creates a path to communication and love. Effacing her father's sexuality, she can reclaim oneness with her mother. This revocation, however, can never transpire because she already exists in the symbolic order.

She continues: "In the picture of me wearing my confirmation dress, I had erased all of myself except for my shoes" (p. 120). These particular shoes specify a tense altercation between Annie

John and her mother. For the ceremony in which she would be received as an adult into the Methodist church, she selected shoes pronounced too risqué by her mother; they sported cut-out sides that exposed the flesh of Annie John's feet, marks of the virginity that her mother sought to protect. Thus she operates in a state of nonclosure, of confusion, even. Her public, religious induction acknowledges imminent adulthood while the reversion to infantilism infusing her sickness signals a refusal of that very acknowledgment. So in the photos her shoes emphatically remain.

An earlier incident throws further light on Annie John's complex relationship to developing sexuality. After a harmless and unexpected conversation with a boy on the way home from school, her mother denounces her as a slut:

> The word "slut" (in patois) was repeated over and over, until suddenly I felt as if I were drowning in a well but instead of the well being filled with water it was filled with the word "slut," and it was pouring in through my eyes, my ears, my nostrils, my mouth. As if to save myself, I turned to her and said, "Well, like father like son, like mother like daughter." (p. 102)

Her mother's accusation threatening Annie John's already fragile identity, her sense of "moral" equality, the word *slut* suffuses her senses. Once again, as in the ocean story and her illness, water scripts betrayal. The seeming irrationality of the mother's charge suggests some overwhelming fear, a link to the mother's adolescent argument with her father—perhaps concerning sexual freedom— her subsequent departure from home and giving birth. In other words the incident might be explained by the fact that Annie John's mother is drawing on personal shame. This hypothesis would also explain why Annie John recollects this particular memory upon seeing her parents in bed. An intimidating sexuality becomes the womb's fluid, her body's fluid. She halts this frightening transformation with words that claim a threatening sexuality as parental heritage. Her father's sexual popularity is pointedly included. They

123

engage each other in emotional pain, then retreat to cope individually with the serious aspersions Annie John has cast:

> At that, everything stopped. The whole earth fell silent. The two black things joined together in the middle of the room separated, hers going to her, mine coming back to me. I looked at my mother. She seemed tired and old and broken. Seeing that, I felt happy and sad at the same time. I soon decided that happy was better, and I was just about to enjoy this feeling when she said, "Until this moment, in my whole life I knew without a doubt that, without any exception, I loved you best," and then she turned her back and started again to prepare the green figs for cooking. (pp. 102–3)

This hurtful statement and the issue of the shoes claim the daughter's right to be as sexually independent as her parents; they defy her mother's warped pronouncement. As markers of the mobility she lacks at the moment, they concurrently pinpoint a dread of the adult world and a means of reentry.

At this point another odd break occurs in the text. When her parent's friend Mr. Nigel, the fisherman, visits her sick bed and laughs at a remark she makes, that laughter spontaneously threatens to engulf her. This complex eruption signals that a gap is opening up: Abject passivity and even degradation are transforming into their opposite, a moment of liberation, her laughter an overmiming, a ridiculing of what she feels they have done to her. She is dissolving her trancelike state through a vivid connection with the everyday world of sight and smell. The invitation to laugh back/ with the fisherman secures relief, offers a vital safety valve that has remained beyond her grasp. This feeling of self-disappearance is accompanied by memories of Mr. Nigel's domestic happiness. Desperately, she leaps on him, fells him to the ground, and garrulously pours out thoughts that crowd her head. Not long after this, grandmother Ma Chess comes:

> [She] settled in on the floor at the foot of my bed, eating and sleeping there, and soon I grew to count on her smells and the

sound her breath made as it went in and out of her body. Sometimes at night, when I would feel that I was locked up in the warm falling soot and could not find my way out, Ma Chess would come into my bed with me and stay until I was myself— whatever that had come to be by then—again. I would lie on my side, curled up like a little comma, and Ma Chess would lie next to me, curled up like a bigger comma, into which I fit. In the daytime, while my mother attended my father, keeping him company as he ate, Ma Chess fed me my food, coaxing me to take mouthful after mouthful. She bathed me and changed my clothes and sheets and did all the other things that my mother used to do. (pp. 125–26)

Annie John has changed herself into a sign of language without voice. This and her grandmother's obeah practices and "ancestral presence" locate her in a historically perilous border area between speech and magic.[12] Note, too, since obeah has been a source of deep contention between slaves and slaveowners, Annie John is using insurrectionary tools to recover and vanquish the likes of her school teacher, Miss Edwards. Through her grandmother Annie John accepts the intervention of an aboriginal world, part of the identity she has fought for. Ma Chess's success affirms the old ways and denies the validity of paternal disapproval of obeah. After this the illness mysteriously vanishes, coinciding with the cessation of the rain. In her first trip outside Annie John establishes her reemergence in the symbolic order:

The sounds I heard didn't pass through me, forming a giant, angry funnel. The things I saw stayed in their places. My mother sat me down under a tree, and I watched a boy she had paid sixpence climb up a coconut tree to get me some coconuts. My mother looked at my pinched, washed-out face and said: "Poor Little Miss, you look so sad." Just at that moment, I was not feeling sad at all. I was feeling how much I never wanted to see a boy climb a coconut tree again . . . how much I never wanted to see the sun shine day in, day out again, how much I never

wanted to see my mother bent over a pot cooking me something
that she felt would do me good when I ate it, how much I never
wanted to feel her long, bony fingers against my cheek again,
how much I never wanted to hear her voice in my ear again,
how much I longed to be in a place where nobody knew a thing
about me and liked me for just that reason, how much the whole
world into which I was born had become an unbearable burden
and I wished I could reduce it to some small thing that I could
hold underwater until it died.   (pp. 127–28)

Through physical illness Annie John has navigated to a place
where she can start over without feeling stifled. She transcends a
shying from independence, now aware that without a sense of
autonomy she will die. Having externalized her distaste for the
fantasy and hypocrisy of her world, she recommences a slow, lop-
sided dance into adulthood. In order to live, she apprehends from
this point on that consciously or not, she has to abandon the island
to dispel its power over her.

Her return to school points to her reinforced, dual position in
the world as insider and outsider. As if play-acting, she dresses
quaintly, beating an inward retreat, while enjoying lavish undue
attention through eccentric behavior; ontologically dislocated, she
buttons up her developing person to hide the mismatch of her
physical, cultural, and psychic subject-positions. With this self-
imposed outsider status Annie John rejects maternal definition, or
rather refashions a sense of pride in her own terms.

Kincaid's inscription of Annie John as a conflicted adolescent
operating in a series of psychodramas is further complicated by
Annie John's resistance to yet another externally imposed construction of herself as a colonial subject. In response Annie John tries to
contextualize pre-1834 colonial life in terms of her own experiences; she revivifies the past by rendering it part of the present.
Leaving aside quarrels with her mother, she attributes her smothered emotions to the consequences of imperial relationships, not
always consciously realized. She refuses to accept assumed episte-

mological "realities," nonsensical formulations of a happy colonial world. Despite teachers' efforts to render her a subject who "works by herself," she revolts.[13]

A book entitled *Roman Britain*, we learn, is a customary school prize as well as an inside joke to anyone who stands outside metropolitan indoctrination: Romans, after all, colonized the British who are still attempting to condition Antiguans to accept imperial ideology. In addition students are reading *A History of the West Indies*, chronicling the colonizer's hagiographical version of Caribbean history, generally unchallenged by the students.[14] Annie John, on the other hand, manifests her awareness of cultural contradictions, refuses to be silenced, and tries to counter the complicities of colonialism and its aftermath. She stresses personal affection for Ruth, "the minister's daughter [who] was such a dunce and came from England and had yellow hair" (p. 73), separate from her political response:

> Perhaps she wanted to be in England, where no one would remind her constantly of the terrible things her ancestors had done; perhaps she had felt even worse when her father was a missionary in Africa. I could see how Ruth felt from looking at her face. Her ancestors had been the masters, while ours had been the slaves. She had such a lot to be ashamed of, and by being with us every day she was always being reminded. We could look everybody in the eye, for our ancestors had done nothing wrong except just sit somewhere, defenseless. Of course, sometimes, what with our teachers and our books, it was hard for us to tell on which side we really now belonged—with the masters or the slaves—for it was all history, it was all in the past, and everybody behaved differently now; all of us celebrated Queen Victoria's birthday, even though she had been dead a long time. But we, the descendants of the slaves, knew quite well what had really happened. (p. 76)

It is no coincidence that Ruth's dunce cap appears to Annie John's conflictual gaze—mocking yet sympathetic—as a regal crown, a synthesis of stupidity and power, not unlike the teacher, Miss Edwards.

Under the picture of a chained-up Columbus in the history text, Annie John has derisively written: "The Great Man Can No Longer Just Get Up and Go." Literally and metaphorically she punctures-punctuates Anglo-Saxon historical reality, attuned to the fact that the Italian adventurer symbolizes all those who have limited, diluted, and even tried to dissolve the political and cultural life of African-Caribbeans.[15] She refuses to sound herself through a white middle-class imaginary. The history lesson that teaches the date of Columbus's "discoveries," we are led to conclude, is neither authentic, nor "all in the past" (p. 76). Since fictions in this culture, she has learned, are called and taught as facts, she plays around with the "facts" and defaces white culture, or rather revises it to bring it more in line with historical events.[16]

Annie John resists received imperial interpretations and a prescribed subject position, however, and functions as the singular representative of historical maroons, slave rebels whose name derives from the Spanish term *cimarron*—wild or untamed. She declines to be mentally manacled by Miss Edwards, whose name conjures up Edward VIII, a king who recently abdicated from a life of duty to a country bent on territorial acquisition. Later the characterization of Miss Edwards as a "bellowing dragon" (to Annie John's knight, presumably) duly underscores the ethnocentric history lessons (p. 78). Annie John battles Miss Edwards's defense of a holy ground that her pupil, proud of a lineage that includes many insurrectionists, rejects with disdain.

Annie John's defiance stems not only from the exercise of power as an adolescent teetering between childhood and adulthood but also from a calculated political rebellion that she attempts to name: her resistance identifies lies about the colonial past, a distorted present, and an unpredictable future. She disrupts the "veneer of family harmony," the advantages of a traditional education.[17] Although she is doubly suppressed and branded as a tough-minded girl and as an ignorant and presumptuous colonized object in the eyes of colonial gazers like Miss Edwards, she refuses obliteration in either sphere.

The choices of other white protagonists differ drastically. Fanny Price refuses to marry Henry Crawford, but in the play-acting episode she conforms to Sir Thomas's values: she does not break the "dead silence" that greet Sir Thomas's account of Antigua. Antoinette personally withdraws in order to cope with post-emancipation resentment and disorder but she is manipulated into marriage with Rochester. She is unable to ally with the black community, and although she identifies with Tia and Christophine emotionally, suicide is the only choice or recourse she can imagine to defeat Rochester and gain agency.[18]

The episode's symbolic significance is finely encapsulated in the punishment the authoritarian Miss Edwards metes out to Annie John. The pupil is commanded to write out *Paradise Lost.*[19] Having located herself on the edge of naughtiness—nuanced opposition to European invasion of the region—she has surrendered primal innocence. Paradise slips away as she recognizes its limitations. We never learn what happens afterward; this indeterminate closure underscores the multiple lost paradises emblemized by Columbus's presence in the Caribbean.

Not by chance the Columbus incident is associated with an earlier escapade in Annie John's life. While Miss Edwards stares at Annie John's deliberate textual defacement, the student flashes back to memories of herself and her friends dancing "on the tombstones of people who had been buried there before slavery was abolished, in 1833." There they would "sit and sing bad songs, use forbidden words, and of course, show each other various parts of our bodies. [Some] would walk up and down on the large tombstones showing off their legs" (pp. 80–81). A ringleader in these exploits, Annie John thus links Columbus and the white student's unforgotten, plantocratic forerunners to historical memory and her self-confident reclamation of unnamed ancestors. The reverberation within her present situation of these earlier audacious acts recalls the narrator's ongoing struggle for personal freedom and political integrity. It stresses, too, the consistency and dialectic of oppression and rebellion.

This episode, which recapitulates the students' wild dance on the graves of slaves, is compounded by telling references to Queen Victoria's birthday, the Union Jack, the presence of Methodist missionaries, and *Jane Eyre*. In identifying with *Jane Eyre*, with whom Annie John has one name (loosely) in common, she betrays certain gaps in her insights about colonial Antigua.[20] For the time being—though this state of affairs changes—Kincaid appears to accept Jane Eyre's struggle with the disruptive presence of the white creole. Hence Annie John accepts this received reading; she does not always see beyond an educational system that trivializes the cultural context of colonized countries. That young Antoinette Cosway (later Bertha Rochester and Jane Eyre's "rival") is a char-acter—the madwoman in the attic, whose "type" would be histori-cally well-known in Antigua—remains unstated. Annie John de-sires and identifies with Jane Eyre's status as an independent female, a solitary, fearless subject who visits Brussels, a cold place and the home of colonizers—the antithesis of Antigua, familiar and de-spised.

Annie John covets Jane Eyre's voluntary exile, her ability to challenge authority. She craves something akin to what appears to her as Jane Eyre's self-crafted autonomy. In ironic reversal Eyre is the exotic outsider and feisty heroine whose gender painfully impedes her.

In the chain of colonial signifiers also appears the name of Enid Blyton, a popular British writer of children's stories. Blyton's pres-ence insinuates something about Annie John's experiences as a black pupil in a colonized society. Long before the writing of *Annie John*, controversy had arisen in Britain over Blyton's ethnocentric texts. In *Here Comes Noddy*, for example, three nasty "golliwogs" mug "poor, little" Noddy.[21] In 1977 Bob Dixon in *Catching Them Young: Sex, Race and Class in Children's Fiction* was one of many British critics to object to Blyton's racist characterizations.[22] Miss Edwards's hagiographical depiction of Columbus as a metropolitan hero bears a second-cousin resemblance to Noddy, pompous white hero of internationally known British children's fiction; the adulation accorded Blyton's characters—like the reverence in which Columbus has been held for centuries—is legend. Blyton's texts were an inevitable component of the storybook repertoire of thousands of British children growing up in the thirties, forties, and fifties. This Blytonian intertextualizing reminds readers of subtle but insistent metropolitan-colonial propaganda about African-Caribbean culture.

Thus Annie John's revolt is indicated through chronological discontinuities that suggest the ubiquity of oppression and indirect revolt in response to colonial lies. Moreover when new information about Annie John in the form of a stream-of-consciousness flashback is introduced in the final chapter as she embarks on her journey to London, these reminiscences enable a rounding out of Annie John's character; its presence through space, time, and place provides some context for what the reader has been invited to see: a young woman claiming agency for herself. The building of Annie John's narrative through association complements the form: sections follow no consistent chronology; rather they track the narrator's circuitous coming to terms with her environment and her final exit. Through cumulative impressions and anecdotes governed by an informing intelligence, Annie John faces down narcissistic colonial myths.

After her metamorphosis following rain and resolution, a postlapsarian Annie John walks to the jetty with her parents. This time the topos of water represents purification of a different sort. She literally will throw herself into deliberate departure (at the jetty-jeté). Having gained a form of freedom, of temporary transcendent agency, she says goodbye and sails for cold London.

Since *Annie John*, Jamaica Kincaid has published another text that permits us to see *Annie John* from enhanced vantage points, especially how colonization constructed Annie John's particular self. Put differently, Jamaica Kincaid recontextualizes in *A Small Place* crucial experiences in Annie John's life. Reasons for Annie John's barely disguised repression, her sense of being trapped within a "First World" modality, for example, become palpably obvious as Kincaid deliberately strips away colonial complicities. The question that inevitably arises about author-narrator and fiction-history relationships is intricate, fraught with the danger of essentialist oppositions. Let me put it this way: In *Annie John* the narrator in "her own" voice plays a large part in conveying what is going on; in *A Small Place* the author forthrightly presents a point of view that demands some mediation. Thus the polemical perspective in *A Small Place* complements and enriches the play of signification in *Annie John*. Kincaid exemplifies her own social conditioning through specifying the constitution of Annie John as an individual. At the same time the many suppressed voices in *A Small Place*—past colonists and present exploiters, for example—convey diverse perspectives. Moreover, the narrator of *Annie John* and Jamaica Kincaid—as she outlines certain experiences in the exposé—have so much undisguisedly in common that the reader is invited to equate them.[23] In that sense Annie John functions as Jamaica Kincaid's avatar. At some points—with respect, say, to understanding parental influence—I avail myself of this invitation.[24]

In *A Small Place* Kincaid denounces Antigua as an island with a legacy of corruption where the mimicking of colonialism has become institutionalized. Part of her diatribe involves identifying the Union Jack and celebrations of Queen Victoria's birthday as corrosive signposts of colonizers, techniques for reinforcing ideological subjection. As such, what lurks suggestively in the innuendos and interstices of *Annie John* are given body and validated through the later narrative.

Additionally, *A Small Place* reilluminates Annie John's father as a glamorous cricketer, a man loved by women long after relationships end. Annie John's mother emerges in a much more focal and public role as a feisty activist who challenges the Antiguan premier himself: "It so happens that in Antigua my mother is fairly notorious for her political opinions" (p. 50). In the earlier text Mrs. John appeared in various guises, often oppositionally to Annie John, so that the adolescent could gradually come to terms with herself, to become, in effect, a writer; she also had to be the mother who extends unconditional love to her daughter. In *A Small Place,* then, the photograph-washing scene in which Annie John sublimates a tumultuous complex of love, anger, and sexual desire takes on a sharper focus. So does her detestation for Columbus. In *A Small Place* tourists are a collective Columbus, new colonists, brash cultural invaders. They are enjoined to forgo customary mindlessness, to accept some responsibility for halting ongoing deterioration. Mediated compassion for someone like blonde Ruth has no place in this uncompromising text. Contemporary prime minister Vere Bird's hegemonic dynasty is post-British collaboration at its worst; the corruption of this administration, Jamaica Kincaid takes pains to point out, originates in a colonizing ethic. *A Small Place* permits us to read Annie John's turmoil as adolescent confusion that often sprang from what she felt but could not name—insecurity, as well as repulsion and fury at being treated as a latter-day colonial object. Yet this is not to deny the intricacy of the reader's position in the trap of fiction-exposé: we move through various forms and stages of identifying with Annie John to viewing Annie John at a greater distance, as an interpellated subject in realpolitik. We see multiple intersecting textualities, "the process of producing [texts] through the transformation of other texts," [25] that help to explain an often invisible, tyrannical world order, the "planned epistemic violence of imperialism." [26]

To put this matter another way, *Annie John* foretells the mature, radical politic of *A Small Place.* At one level *A Small Place* is *Annie John,* part 2. Kincaid's disclosures validate Annie John's dimly felt sense of being indoctrinated and condescended to. Earlier disquiet becomes withering sarcasm. In yet one more sense *Annie John* problematizes *A Small Place,* enables us to see that no last word exists. Together the texts help to reconceptualize contemporary

definitions of female sexuality, motherhood, and race/gender intersections through the gaze of an African-Caribbean woman: [27] "A
full literary reinscription cannot easily flourish in the imperialist
fracture or discontinuity, covered over by an alien legal system
masquerading as Law as such, an alien ideology established as only
Truth, and a set of human sciences busy establishing the 'native' as
self-consolidating other." [28]

As the main topos of *A Small Place*, colonialism marks Kincaid's
candid characterizations of Horatio Nelson, Sir Francis Drake, and
other renowned heroes of British naval history as "English maritime
criminals" (p. 24). In *A Small Place* the slippery, dissolving paradise
of *Annie John* could be only a fantastic memory of childhood in
which a sophisticated yet horrified narrator pointedly intertwines
contemporary abominations with past atrocities:

> You must not wonder what exactly happened to the contents of
> your lavatory when you flushed it. You must not wonder where
> your bath water went when you pulled out the stopper. You must
> not wonder what happened when you brushed your teeth. Oh, it
> might all end up in the water you are thinking of taking a swim
> in; the contents of your lavatory might, just might, graze gently
> against your ankle as you wade carefree in the water, as you see,
> in Antigua, there is no proper sewage-disposal system. But the
> Caribbean Sea is very big and the Atlantic Ocean is even bigger;
> it would amaze even you to know the number of black slaves this
> ocean has swallowed up. When you sit down to eat your delicious
> meal, it's better than you don't know that most of what you are
> eating came off a plane from Miami. And before it got on a
> plane in Miami, who knows where it came from? A good guess is
> that it came from a place like Antigua first, where it was grown
> dirt-cheap, went to Miami, and came back. There is a world of
> something in this, but I can't go into it right now.
>
> (pp. 13–14)

Unilaterally excoriating the reigning Antiguan dynasty of Vere
Bird, Kincaid exposes endless vestiges of colonialism. She mocks

the idea of a "British God" (p. 9); she ridicules tourists who think Antiguans are specially bonded with nature or act as monkeys just out of trees (p. 29). Tourists themselves are denounced categorically—each one is "an ugly, empty thing, a stupid thing, a piece of rubbish" (p. 17) who circulates in a malevolent miniworld. In response Kincaid asserts: "This empire business was all wrong" (p. 23). Such unabounding ire radiates elsewhere, as in "There is a world of something in this, but I can't go into it right now" (p. 14) and "Do you even try to understand why people like me cannot get over the past, cannot forgive and cannot forget?" (p. 26).

Incontestable denunciation in *A Small Place* has replaced the implicit jabs of *Annie John*: "We were taught the names of the Kings of England. In Antigua, the 24th of May was a holiday— Queen Victoria's official birthday."[29] One of the colonized coerced into ostensible celebration, she specifies the perniciousness of "bad post-colonial education" (p. 43) and "an appropriate obsession with slavery." Black teenagers, she argues, "generally [make] asses of themselves. What surprised me most about them was not how familiar they were with the rubbish of North America—compared to the young people of my generation, who were familiar with the rubbish of England" (pp. 43–44).

> In Antigua, people speak of slavery as if it had been a pageant full of large ships sailing on the blue water, the large ships filled up with human cargo—their ancestors, they got off, they were forced to work under conditions that were cruel and inhuman, they were beaten, they were murdered, they were sold, their children were taken from them and these separations lasted forever, there were many other bad things, and then suddenly the whole thing came to an end in something called emancipation. Then they speak of emancipation itself as if it happened just the other day, not over one hundred and fifty years ago. The word "emancipation" is used so frequently, it is as if it, emancipation, were a contemporary occurrence, something everybody is familiar with. (pp. 54–55)

Not to put a fine point on it, Kincaid holds colonialism responsible for everything noxious that she hints at and intuits in *Annie
John*:

> Have you ever wondered why it is that all we seem to have
> learned from you is how to corrupt our societies and how to be
> tyrants? You will have to accept that this is mostly your fault. . . .
> You imprisoned people. You robbed people. You opened your
> own banks and you put our money in them. The accounts were
> in your name. The banks were in your name. There must have
> been some good people among you, but they stayed home. And
> that is the point. That is why they are good. They stayed home.
> But still, when you think about it, you must be a little sad. The
> people like me, finally, after years and years of agitation, made
> deeply moving and eloquent speeches against the wrongness of
> your domination over us, and then finally, after the mutilated
> bodies of you, your wife, and your children were found in your
> beautiful and spacious bungalow at the edge of your rubber plan-
> tation—found by one of your many house servants (none of it
> was ever yours; it was never, ever yours)—you say to me, "Well,
> I wash my hands of all of you, I am leaving now."   (pp. 34–36)

Together these texts build a heady opposition to past and present
Antigua. *Annie John* and *A Small Place* produce a "strategic formation"; in a limited way these exposés "acquire mass, density, and
referential power among themselves and thereafter in the culture at
large."[30] They construct themselves as a textual other, as a counterdiscourse to dominant culture and ideology. As an African-
Caribbean writer Kincaid speaks to and from the position of the
other. Not only does she identify confrontations along race/gender
axes, she unmasks "the results of those distortions internalized
within our consciousness of ourselves and one another."[31]

Kincaid signals the degeneration of the public library as the
transcendent symbol of outsider devastation, the silencing of a
cultural institution that has traditionally been one of the sole and
free instructors of the people. It has rendered the people voice-

less:[32] "But what I see [ironically at a royal procession] is the millions of people, of whom I am just one, made orphans: no motherland, no fatherland, no gods, no mounds of earth for holy ground, no excess of love which might lead to the things that an excess of love sometimes brings, and worst and most painful of all, no tongue" (p. 31). Library books, which Annie John felt guilty about stealing, are resymbolized as critical cultural items that have been commandeered by an imperial culture to deprive former slaves of self-education. In Marlene Nourbese Philip's words: "Silence welcomes the hungry word."[33] Colonizers and their servants, not Annie John, were and are the thieves who try to cut off, as colonizers of old, the people's tongue.[34] Jamaica Kincaid sounds the voice of the people into the void. A postcolonial narrative and reevaluated site, *A Small Place* demystifies Annie John's bewilderment about unnamed oppositions.

In the novel bearing her name Annie John charts a complex journey into adolescence, a slow initiation into adulthood; she discerns simultaneous oppressions but refuses to "become" a lady or be a tool of surrogate colonizers. Instead she devises a means to independence and challenges readers to reexamine old models of what autonomy means for women.[35] She tries to mediate so many different representatives of herself that she speaks in several voices, including a silent or a self-silenced voice. Disrespectful in society's eyes, she records a coming to power that demystifies (to herself, at least) colonial and gender alienation, the stifling realities engendered by a predator's legacy. Initially, until the age of twelve, she assimilates wholesale the given "master narratives" about family, education, and culture. Then she backs off to take a closer look and eventually withdraws. She does not know how else to face cultural worlds and hegemonic practices that she cannot reconcile; she has few tools to cope with such a complicated subjectivity. The seemingly neutral zone of rain becomes the sign of social and psychic self-alienation, an agonized splitting from childhood, her last farewell.[36] In declining to internalize the given epistemology of appearance and reality, she forges a unique identity. Struggle, then, is at the core, is the core of *Annie John*. Having forcibly cracked open the hitherto homogenized, gendered, and colonial space, she maintains herself shakily on several planes, her reconciliations restless and incomplete. Fighting on public and private fronts, Annie John negotiates her way through alienation to choice. She sails off to wrestle an elusive subjectivity and chart an adult identity.

Jamaica Kincaid's subsequent jeremiad about Antigua, *A Small Place*, evokes the repressed subtexts of *Annie John* by openly indicting historical domination, recontextualizing earlier hesitant responses to cultural role-playing, and encoding insensitive tourists as updates of Christopher Columbus. The villains of Annie John's adolescent naïveté—particularly her mother—are reconfigured more authentically to include their status as subalterns in Antiguan society; contemporary leadership is forthrightly condemned. Kincaid's recognition that colonialism is to blame for social corruption only slightly mitigates her rage at the present state of affairs. However, at the end of *Annie John* these articulations are barely a whisper. Annie John's surname, resonating with biblical overtones and sexual innuendo, symbolizes the creative potential she has frequently expressed, the beginnings she has recreated with words, her struggle between male and female modalities. Embarking on the journey to London is simultaneously the end of adolescence and the beginning of her future life as a cultural demystifier.

Conclusion

Even in those books without identifiably political content, a judgement is being made
and invariably it is a judgement against the
valuing of *things* and for the valuing of *people*.
There is a sense in which the major concerns
of women's writing can be reduced (or ex-
panded) to these most simple, essential considerations. Issues of race and class, of gender,
of slavery, of history, of persons and person-
hood and of oppression, certainly turn on this
valuing.

—*Her True-True Name,*
Pamela Mordecai and
Betty Wilson, eds., p. xiii

Throughout this book I have shown how authors have engaged in
a variety of conversations about colonial and gender relations.
These conversations have in part depended on the obvious: chronology and geography, but largely on various levels of privileged
cultural positions and ideological awareness—that is, on authors'

139

political perspectives regarding patriarchal relations and on slavery in general and abolition and emancipation in particular. Attitudes about class and sexuality, moreover, are an integral part of these vantage points on race and gender.

Living and writing in London in Dissenting intelligentsia circles in the aftermath of the North American, French, and San Domingo revolutions, Mary Wollstonecraft was incensed about the absence of mainly white middle-class women's rights. Her constituency, she argued, should be accorded full citizenship.[1] However, in its configuration of gender, sexuality, and its colonial referents, A *Vindication of the Rights of Men* indicates that Wollstonecraft is also committed to ending slavery. Hence she presents her argument in A *Vindication of the Rights of Woman* through the lens of race, thereby affirming her political engagement with both issues.

Among upper-class Methodist circles in Antigua, Anne Hart Gilbert and Elizabeth Hart Thwaites dealt the heaviest blows they appropriately could against slavery and female exploitation, not like Mary Wollstonecraft in the name of formal, legal, human rights, but as a spiritual consideration. Thus the Hart sisters were the earliest African-Caribbean writers in English to discuss women and emancipation—as opposed to the logically prior step of abolition. In that sense they set their texts in transatlantic dialogue with the second *Vindication*. However, although the texts exchange different multicultural dialogues according to their variant contexts, they do intersect on the question of rights. Mary Wollstonecraft polemicizes as a lone propagandist and gets dubbed a "hyena in petticoats" for her trouble. Elizabeth Hart Thwaites is brought before the Antiguan Privy Council, not for propagandizing but for the possibly improper distribution of funds to the "Poor and Distressed Negroes of Antigua," the name given to the organization set up by British antislavery auxiliaries.

Openly committed to abolition within the Methodist Society as Elizabeth Hart Thwaites's *History of Methodism* avows, the sisters represent themselves in public as educators rather than propagandists. Given the precariousness of their social situation as African-

Antiguan Methodists within a white-ruled, nominally Anglican colony, they negotiate the tightrope between moral instruction and political polemic very surefootedly. As they persist in teaching slaves to read and acquire skills for the labor market, the power of the white plantocracy indirectly diminishes.

In their subtle politic of resistance to the patriarchal and colonial establishment, Anne Hart Gilbert and Elizabeth Hart Thwaites nonetheless act for all black Antiguans, including, in the official designation, "free colored" women like themselves. They are especially attentive to "fallen" girls and women, their code for females who are forcibly abused in a plantocracy that endorses white male sexual permissiveness. Acting as an informal opposition to reckless sexual license, they pay particular attention to female morals.

Furthermore, they initiate literacy programs for related reasons. Because of their class connections they are aware of intense debates over abolition and emancipation in Britain; they see the writing on slavery's wall. Hence through moral instruction they prepare thousands of enslaved African-Antiguans for formal entry into a heterogeneous waged market economy. As forerunners of liberation theologists like Kortright Davis from contemporary Antigua, they agitate for freedom and justice with the means at their disposal.

Jane Austen's representations of gender and colonial relations incline across Mary Wollstonecraft's, Anne Hart Gilbert's, and Elizabeth Hart Thwaites's in several ways. First, Austen traverses Mary Wollstonecraft's overt concern for women's legal rights with a discussion of Fanny Price's "inferior" status and the discrepant response it attracts; then, imbricated in that discussion is the nuanced suggestion that Fanny Price's exploited status, her cultural colonization, and relative lack of choice in England might overlap at some points with the status of silenced slaves on the island where Sir Thomas travels to check up on things; third, the modified network of hegemonic control in *Mansfield Park* echoes notorious plantocratic domestic and labor relations.

At the same time the work (and worth) of Anne Hart Gilbert and Elizabeth Hart Thwaites do not figure in *Mansfield Park*, not because the text is not *about* African-Antiguan life but because *Mansfield Park* is, in part, precisely about that. Life at Mansfield Park crucially depends on slavery, on the success of fictional Sir Thomas's plantations. Although no word as vulgar as *plantocrat* taints his mouth, he is one of those very absentee landlords whose slaves Anne Hart Gilbert and Elizabeth Hart Thwaites are teaching. Or perhaps they are not teaching very many of the "real material subjects" of Anglican plantocrats since the instruction of slaves—as Sir Thomas knows from his conversations with upper-class British administrators and white Antiguan creoles—is often forbidden.[2]

In *Wide Sargasso Sea* a critical political act has occurred—namely, emancipation—that shifts the discourse about rights, retaliation, and resistance to another level. This distinctive liberation produces a very different mise-en-scène. A new fictional brand of Sir Thomas, corporealized in Rochester, spars with now freed African-Antiguan men, women, and children. The special role and burden of women's sexual subordination is rearticulated. The dispossessed, multiply-named white creole Antoinette Cosway becomes the symbolic object of struggle, the site of contestation through whom and over whom the battle for future state power is locked. In that sense Jean Rhys tells or retells the tale of post-emancipation Antiguan history from the point of view of members of the former dominant class. She projects what might happen (what has happened) into her own day.

Put another way, Jean Rhys "photographs" for posterity early frames of the dual battle for hegemonic control of Dominica and concurrently records the demise of a certain section of the white ruling class. Thus Rhys's intervention in the post-emancipation struggle is early and late; it constitutes a bridging act. *Wide Sargasso Sea* cannot be told—as *Mansfield Park* was told—without the active presence of women resembling Anne Hart Gilbert and Elizabeth Hart Thwaites, historical African-Antiguan subjects who refuse to take metropolitan guff any longer. Diversely empowered African-Dominicans run rings around the unnamed male protagonist and

Antoinette Cosway, the former colonizer and her usurper, no match for a post-emancipation community ready for self-government. They expose the close relation of sexuality to politics under colonial rule and its aftermath. Like the Hart sisters, though in a different guise, the black community resists white domination. *Wide Sargasso Sea* is another text that dissolves tidy closure. It is no accident, either, as previous texts have indicated, that the African-Caribbean presence, in this case the presences of Christophine and Tia, are determining ones in the activities of Coulibri, Granbois, and Thornfield Hall, for that matter. In fictional terms African-Caribbean women appropriate rights that Mary Wollstonecraft and the Hart sisters directly and indirectly demanded for women. They eschew a pre-emancipation existence, refusing the "dead silence" of the slaves to whom Sir Thomas refers. Gynocentric participants in an evolving culture, they exert agency.

Growing up during the last days of colonialism in Antigua, Jamaica Kincaid glosses all the previous texts through *Annie John*. In *A Small Place*, however, she announces a different combative strategy: overt textual resistance. Jamaica Kincaid crystallizes her predecessors' usage of texts as weapons. She shows the jeopardized plight of legally freed but still psychologically and sexually colonized women. A fictional synthesizer, whether consciously or not, Jamaica Kincaid inherits the consequences of emancipation and grows up in a country wrestling to free itself from Britain. While Jean Rhys actively composed *Wide Sargasso Sea*, Annie John/ Jamaica Kincaid was living in colonial, soon to be a partially independent, Antigua.

In a sense Jamaica Kincaid gives voice to the continuum of messages in all the other texts by showing where they fit, overlap, slip out, spill over. She puts a new spin on women writers' implicit and explicit textual representations of the relation of women to colonialism and postcolonialism. She underwrites the uncommon role and responsibility of women's sexual as well as political and cultural subordination. Annie John will not be fashioned into a lady and indoctrinated in colonial history. Like the Hart sisters she deliberately sites herself outside the context of the colonizers, a subject in her own right, resisting indoctrination.

Kincaid, that is, puts an end to silence or to the idea that though a great deal does not seem to have been done (vide *A Small Place*), things will remain the same. Jamaica Kincaid's more autobiographical analysis of cultural imperialism in *A Small Place* exemplifies her resoluteness as an oppositional voice, regardless of consequences. In *A Small Place* Jamaica Kincaid publicly proclaims that the differences between colonial and postcolonial Antigua astound her. She denounces the fact that the same demeaning roles still obtain for women, that the matrix of past gender and colonial relations has shifted only slightly and she, for one, has had enough. More than that, she will try to alter the situation. Through *Annie John* and *A Small Place,* that is, Jamaica Kincaid enacts a politic of engagement, of political exhortation to others to take up cudgels for a future, richer self-determination. Kincaid ends on an uncompromising note of anger, almost on a call for popular agency. She asks people denied full civil rights to claim these rights. The ambiguities of conflicts and negotiations articulated by Mary Wollstonecraft, Jane Austen, Anne Hart Gilbert, Elizabeth Hart Thwaites, and Jean Rhys are voiced once again and demand to be heard, but in a different time and in a small place. Jamaica Kincaid wants the battle for rights to be waged collectively. The dialogue and the struggle move to a different level.

Notes

2. Mary Wollstonecraft and the Problematic of Slavery

1. C. L. R. James, *The Black Jacobins*, p. ix.

2. Mary Wollstonecraft, *Thoughts on the Education of Daughters with Reflections on Female Conduct, in the more Important Duties of Life* (London: Johnson, 1787), p. 63.

3. Wollstonecraft, *Mary: A Fiction* (London: 1788, reprinted as *Mary: A Fiction* and *The Wrongs of Woman*, edited and introduced by Gary Kelly), p. 49. Writers as diverse as Katherine Philips, the Duchess of Newcastle, Aphra Behn, Mrs. Taylor, Lady Chudleigh, Sarah Fyge Field Egerton, Anne Finch, the Countess of Winchilsea, Elizabeth Rowe, Elizabeth Tollett, and many more frequently employed the metaphor of slavery to express the subjugation of women; marriage was far and away the foremost situation in which women described themselves or other women as enslaved. Note also that Wollstonecraft refers to the Spartans' perpetual subjugation in Lacedaemonian society of the Helots, state serfs bound to the soil with no political rights. Shimron, *Late Sparta*, p. 96; Michell, *Sparta*, pp. 75–84; MacDowell, *Spartan Law*, pp. 23–25, 31–42.

4. Coupland, *The British Anti-Slavery Movement*, p. 68.

5. Clarkson, *African Slave-Trade*, vol. 1 (London: Longman, Hurst, Rees, and Orme, 1808), pp. 276–85 and passim.

6. Craton, *Sinews of Empire*, especially ch. 5.

145

2. Mary Wollstonecraft and Slavery

7. Sunstein, A Different Face, p. 171.

8. Olaudah Equiano, The Interesting Narrative of the Life of Olaudah Equiano or Gustavus Vassa, the African. Written by Himself, vol. 1 (London, printed and sold by the author, 1789; reprinted as Equiano's Travels, edited by Paul Edwards).

9. Wollstonecraft, The Female Reader.

10. Wollstonecraft, The Female Reader, "The History of Inkle and Yarico," pp. 29–31; "Negro Woman," p. 171; and "On Slavery" (from The Task), pp. 321–22.

11. Wollstonecraft, The Analytical Review . . . . (London: Johnson, vol. 5, September 1789, pp. 98–103; October 1789, pp. 227–32; Appendix to Vol. 5, pp. 574–77).

12. Richard Price, A Discourse on the Love of Our Country. . . ., 2d ed. (Dublin: Chamberlaine, 1790), p. 55.

13. Edmund Burke, Reflections on the Revolution in France (London: 1790; reprint New York: Doubleday, 1961).

14. Wollstonecraft, The Rights of Men, 2d ed. (London: Johnson, 1790). All references are to this edition.

15. Tomalin, Life and Death of Mary Wollstonecraft.

16. Wollstonecraft, The Rights of Woman (London: Johnson, 1792), p. x. All references are to this edition.

17. Wollstonecraft, The Rights of Men, p. 76.

18. Ibid., pp. 45, 59.

19. Catharine Macaulay Graham, Letters of Education. With Observation on Religious and Metaphysical Subjects, introduction by Gina Luria (New York and London: Garland, 1974). For a wide-ranging discussion about the relationship between feminism and individualism during the Enlightenment, see Fox-Genovese, Feminism Without Illusions, particularly pp. 1–10, 124, 141.

20. Ferguson, First Feminists, p. 399.

21. Ibid., pp. 403–4.

22. Christian Gotthilf Salzmann, Elements of Morality for the Use of Children (London: Johnson, 1790).

23. Craton, Sinews of Empire, p. 261.

24. C. L. R. James, The Black Jacobins, p. ix.

25. Klingberg, Anti-Slavery, pp. 88–95.

26. Wollstonecraft, The Rights of Women, pp. 37, 138.

27. Vicesimus Knox, "On the Fear of Appearing Singular," no. 5 in Essays Moral and Literary: 21–22. A New Edition in Two Volumes (London: Dilly, 1782).

28. Wollstonecraft, The Rights of Woman, pp. 186–87. Wollstonecraft does not hold exclusively to those attitudes, however. In the Analytical Review somewhat later, she argues, for example, that Hottentot people act in harmony with their situation. Analytical Review (May 1797) 25: 466.

2. Mary Wollstonecraft and Slavery

29. David Hume, "Of National Character," *The Philosophical Works of David Hume*, 4 vols. (London, 1898), 3: 252. The essay was first published in 1742, but the passage quoted was added as a footnote in the edition of 1753–54. See also M. Cook. "Jean Jacques Rousseau and the Negro," *Journal of Negro History* (July 1936) 21: 294–303, cited in Philip D. Curtin, *The Image of Africa: British Ideas and Action, 1780–1850* (Madison: University of Wisconsin Press, 1964), p. 42.

30. For example, as a slave in Bermuda and then in Antigua, Mary Prince is attacked by a vitriolic writer (name unknown) in a proslavery newspaper article. The trunk of her only worldly possessions (containing unspecified items), which she took from her owner when she left, is exaggerated by this writer as "several trunks of clothes" to suggest excess vanity and even prostitution. "She at length left his house, taking with her several trunks of clothes and about 40 guineas in money, which she had saved in Mr. Wood's service" (Zuill, *Bermuda Sampler, 1815–1850*, p. 144).

31. Attentiveness to appearance, across cultures and stemming from different origins, infuriates Wollstonecraft. The fact that her own appearance is negatively commented upon at this time suggests itself as a factor in her reaction. Apparently she spruced herself up when she became infatuated with Henry Fuseli, the Swiss painter. See Flexner, *Mary Wollstonecraft*, pp. 138–39.

32. For Wollstonecraft's views on Eros and her anger at women as sexual objects of men, see Kathleen Blake, *Love and the Woman Question in Victorian Literature: The Art of Self-Postponement* (Totowa, N.J.: Barnes & Noble, 1983), p. 103–4.

33. Wollstonecraft, *The Rights of Woman*, pp. 82–83.

34. Cora Kaplan, *Sea Changes: Essays on Culture and Feminism* (London: Verso, 1986), p. 48.

35. Hannah More's opinions on women constitute one of Mary Wollstonecraft's significant textual silences, but most notably in the second *Vindication*. Wollstonecraft vociferously applauds women's assuming more prominent sociocultural roles, she implicitly intertextualizes More's opposition to this advice. See also Sylvia Harestark Myers, *The Bluestocking Circle: Women, Friendship, and the Life of the Mind in Eighteenth-Century England* (Oxford: Clarendon Press, 1990), pp. 260–62.

36. *Analytical Review* (December 1788) 2: 431–39. See also Samuel Stanhope Smith, *An Essay on the Causes of the Variety of Complexion and Figure in the Human Species* (2d ed., New Brunswick, N.J.: J. Simpson; New York: Williams and Whiting, 1810). Reissued as *An Essay on the Causes of Variety . . .* , Winthrop D. Jordan, ed. (Cambridge, Mass.: Harvard University Press, 1965).

37. However, despite Wollstonecraft's argument that ethnic differences are due to climate and social conditions à la Stanhope Smith and her unilateral

commitment to abolition, she remains ambivalent about black equality. Her acceptance of a system that operates on the differential between owners and workers and on the basis of certain assumptions about European superiority can never square with an absolute human liberation. Everything is measured against the model of a European society that regards African society as the other. Wollstonecraft may Eurocentrically contend that people in other cultures would be smart and civilized if they were raised as she was, but her review of Olaudah Equiano's narratives gives the lie even to that belief: "We shall only observe, that if these volumes do not exhibit extraordinary intellectual powers, sufficient to wipe off the stigma, yet the activity and ingenuity, which conspicuously appear in the character of Gustavus, [i.e., Equiano] place him on a par with the general mass of men, who fill the subordinate factions in a more civilized society than that which he was thrown into at his birth." *Analytical Review* (May 1789) 4: 28.

38. The writings of such laboring-class women as Mary Collier, as well as slave Phillis Wheatley, are only two examples of people from dominated communities whose writings had to be "authenticated" by others in eighteenth-century Britain.

39. Wollstonecraft, *Analytical Review* (May 1789) 4: 28.

40. Equiano, *Interesting Narrative of His Life . . . Written by Himself*, p. 69.

41. Ibid., p. 121.

42. Wollstonecraft, *The Female Reader*, p. 31. Aside from her commentary on Equiano's and Yarico's experiences, among others, Wollstonecraft also recognizes other ways that sexuality oppresses white women. She had dealt on a personal level with her sister Eliza's postpartum depression by effecting Eliza's separation from her husband, Hugh Skeys. She felt, it seems, as if Skeys were responsible for her sister's condition; she treated him more or less as a male predator, a villain of sorts. At the same time, *The Rights of Woman* appeared at a time in her life when she was immersed in a difficult personal situation; she was discovering that the choices open to a woman who wants to work and to love were very limited.

43. Wollstonecraft, *The Rights of Woman*, p. 144.

44. Jordan, *White Over Black*, pp. 150–54.

45. Wollstonecraft, *The Rights of Woman*, pp. 82–83.

46. Ibid., p. 17.

47. Remember, too, that psychologically, Wollstonecraft's attack on male sexuality could mark a displaced attack on Fuseli, whose male sexuality has engendered inner turmoil. Mary Poovey's argument that *"men's* [and not women's] insatiable appetites" are Wollstonecraft's target is worth considering in the light of her passion for the Swiss painter. Mary Poovey, *The Proper Lady and the Woman Writer: Ideology as Style in the Works of Mary Wollstonecraft, Mary Shelley, and Jane Austen* (Chicago: University of Chicago Press, 1984), pp. 71–76 and passim. See also discussions of displacement in Anna Freud,

Ego, pp. 155–56 and passim. On a somewhat related note with respect to sexuality, the Jacobins often resembled the Evangelicals. See, for example, a discussion of Mary Wollstonecraft's Maria in Butler, *Jane Austen and the War of Ideas*, pp. 45–47.

3. The Hart Sisters: Early African-Caribbean Educators and the "Thirst for Knowledge"

1. Box, *Memoir of John Gilbert*, pp. 6–7, p. 292. Note that the Reverend William Box was a Wesleyan Methodist who had been in Jamaica during the insurrection. The Hart sisters knew the strategic role that missionaries and religious instructors played in slave societies. Horsford, *A Voice*, p. 126.

2. Oddly enough, except for son-in-law John Gilbert in his autobiography, no one mentions that Barry Conyers Hart, a man from a politically well-known white family, was a "man of colour." Box, *Memoir of John Gilbert*, p. 22.

3. Goveia, *Slave Society*, p. 223.

4. Green, *British Slave Emancipation* (Oxford: Clarendon Press, 1976), p. 17.

5. Elizabeth Hart Thwaites's *History of Methodism* is addressed to the Reverend Richard Pattison, who was first a missionary on Nevis. See Findlay and Holdsworth, *The History of the Wesleyan Methodist Missionary Society*, 2: 55. They add of Pattison: "a young man of excellent sense and fidelity, who did good service in the West Indies while his health lasted." In the London Methodist Missionary Archives, the Reverend Richard Pattison is mentioned as Anne Gilbert's correspondent in the *History of Methodism*. The sisters' holographs of the *History of Methodism* are in the Methodist Missionary Society Archives in London. For the texts in their entirety and related materials and original manuscripts of the Hart sisters and their relatives, see Ferguson, ed., *The Hart Sisters*. Note also an extensive discussion of the free colored community in Goveia, *Slave Society*, pp. 80–83 and passim.

6. Findlay and Holdsworth, *Wesleyan Methodist Missionary Society*, p. 140.

7. Goveia, *Slave Society*, p. 290.

8. Horsford, *A Voice*, pp. 160–61.

9. Ibid., p. 153; Findlay and Holdsworth, *Wesleyan Methodist Missionary Society*, pp. 30–31.

10. Drescher, *Capitalism and Antislavery*, p. 120.

11. Horsford, *A Voice*, p. 195.

12. Felicity A. Nussbaum, *The Autobiographical Subject: Gender and Ideology in Eighteenth-Century England* (Baltimore: The Johns Hopkins University Press, 1989), p. 89 and passim.

13. Anne Hart Gilbert, *History of Methodism*, p. 11.

14. No recent book exists that specifically documents the history of Antigua in the decades before emancipation. In her extensive study, *Slave Society*, Goveia documents some important history and statistics about slave society. Other important data can be culled from a valuable variety of often religion-based histories and studies of the island mentioned in these notes.

15. Drescher, *Capitalism and Antislavery*, p. 114.

16. Box, *Memoir of John Gilbert*, p. 85. Born in St. Johns, Antigua, in 1767, John Gilbert was apprenticed at fourteen to a naval storekeeper. Seriously ill in 1784 he was nursed back to health by the wife of John Baxter, a shipwright and influential Wesleyan preacher.

17. Ibid., p. 23. The Antiguan historian, Frances Lanaghan, speaks explicitly and at some length about prejudice on the island, including the treatment of the Gilberts. See Lanaghan, *Antigua and the Antiguans*, 1: 177–82 and passim. I thank Desmond Nicholson for supplying me with Frances Lanaghan's correct name. (The title page has no name, but the book is generally attributed to a Mrs. Lanaghan. Desmond Nicholson discovered her full name by writing to her relatives.)

18. Lanaghan, *Antigua and the Antiguans*, 1: 179.

19. Anne Hart Gilbert, *History of Methodism*, p. 19.

20. Ibid., p. 20. For an update of Anne Hart Gilbert's refusal to deny any positive features of obeah, see Davis, *Emancipation Still Comin'*, pp. 54–55. In Gilbert's day it was much less easy to incorporate old practices in light of univocal Methodist beliefs.

21. Ibid., p. 21. Note also, perhaps to offset her criticism, Anne Gilbert emphasizes the role played by Mary Gilbert, widow of Francis Gilbert, another affirmation of female spiritual solidarity.

22. Ibid., p. 21. Note also the lengths to which Anne Hart Gilbert will go in her desire to provide literacy, spiritual instruction, and a general sense of communication among members of the black community. Joseph Sturge, a well-known British antislavery activist who traveled to Antigua in 1837 to see how post-emancipation slaves were being treated, stated that Gilbert held meetings in the dark so that slaves who had only one set of clothes (usually dirty) could attend meetings without shame. See Sturge and Harvey, *The West Indies in 1837*, p. 36.

23. Ibid., pp. 7–8; Goveia, *Slave Society*, pp. 7–8.

24. Gilbert, *History of Methodism*, pp. 9–10.

25. Ibid., p. 19. Propagating orthodox Methodist practices, John Baxter seeks out black spiritual leaders and makes sure that converted people conform to John Wesley's desired terminology in using the word *chapel*, not *meetinghouse* or *church*. For the condition of Methodism when Baxter arrived in Antigua, see Goveia, *Slave Society*, p. 289–90.

26. Box, *Memoir of John Gilbert*, p. 87; Horsford, *A Voice*, p. 200. On his official travels to oversee the implementation of the Emancipation Act, British

abolitionist Joseph Sturge offers a Methodist's retrospective view of Anne Hart Gilbert's charitable work: "We went, also, to see the 'Refuge for Female Orphans,' an interesting and most useful institution, which is dependent on the English 'Ladies' Society.' It was declining for want of attention; its chief support had been Mrs. Gilbert, an excellent lady of colour, now dead." Sturge and Harvey, *The West Indies in 1837*, p. 36. Another contemporary discussion of the foundation of these societies appears in Thome and Kimball, *Emancipation in the West Indies*, p. 113ff.

27. Horsford, *A Voice*, p. 197; Box, *Memoir of John Gilbert*, p. 37.

28. Hart, "Letter from Miss Elizabeth Hart to a Friend," 1794, in Horsford, *A Voice*, p. 18. The page references in all subsequent citations of this letter refer to Horsford's book. The holograph of this letter is in the Methodist Missionary Society Archives, London. See also note 1.

29. Ferguson, ed. *The History of Mary Prince*, pp. 8–9.

30. Hart, *History of Methodism*, p. 4; see note 1.

31. Ibid., p. 10.

32. "Letter from Elizabeth Hart to Elizabeth Lynch," quoted in Horsford, *A Voice*, p. 198.

33. Horsford, *A Voice*, p. 203.

34. Findlay and Holdsworth, *Wesleyan Methodist Missionary Society*, p. 141.

35. Hart, *History of Methodism*, p. 6.

36. Ibid. In speaking of the condition of slaves and the need for education, Elizabeth Hart Thwaites introduces commentary, as her sister Anne did about the specific role played by the colonial order. On one occasion, for example, she stated that the white ruling class continued "wilfully blind" in their claim that slaves are "much better off than the poor Europeans." Elizabeth Hart, "Letter . . . to a Friend," p. 10.

37. For discussions of pidgin and the relationship of its usage to power relations, see Suzanne Romaine, *Pidgin and Creole Languages* (London and New York: Longman, 1988), pp. 72–75 and passim.

38. Hart, *History of Methodism*, p. x.

39. Hart, "Letter . . . to a Friend," p. 12.

40. Box, *Memoir of John Gilbert*, pp. 86–87.

41. Horsford, *A Voice*, p. 188. Note also how collectively the sisters worked and pursued their particular educational concerns. In the 1820s the Gilberts apparently took over the responsibility of superintending Sunday schools from Elizabeth Hart Thwaites. Teaching had ceased at the Gilberts' house in 1817 at the end of the Napoleonic wars when the Royal Navy reduced its base— and hence John Gilbert's position—in English Harbour. The Gilberts moved their work to St. Johns but then returned to English Harbour in 1821 when John Gilbert was appointed naval storekeeper. By this time the Honorable Lady Grey, patroness of the English Harbour Sunday School Society, had been providing Methodist schoolroom space for four years. She appointed Anne

Hart Gilbert superintendent of the girls' section of the school. See Horsford, *A Voice*, p. 201.

42. Roy Porter, *English Society in the Eighteenth Century* (New York: Penguin, 1982), p. 305. Note also that the educational organizing undertaken by the sisters coincided with a time of "moral backsliding" in Antigua, as noted by the missionaries. See Findlay and Holdsworth, *Wesleyan Methodist Missionary Society*, 2: 136 and passim.

43. Manuscript in box 11, item 12 at the School of Oriental and African Studies, University of London, Methodist Missionary Correspondence, extract from a letter written by Charles Thwaites, Antigua, August 25, n.d. The full text of this letter appears in Ferguson, ed., *The Hart Sisters*.

44. Horsford, *A Voice*, p. 203.

45. Lanaghan, *Antigua and the Antiguans*, 1: 316–21. Note, too, that Charles Thwaites peppers his journal with tales of their philanthropic activities regarding "fallen" women, backsliding, and young people's conversion. The holograph of these journals appears in the Methodist Missionary Society Archives, London. See note 1. In all, the Thwaiteses ministered to sixty estates in addition to a night school in their own house consisting of eighty to one hundred children. A further discussion of Thwaites's role appears in Thome and Kimball, *Emancipation*, p. 123ff.

46. Lanaghan, *Antigua and the Antiguans*, 1: 318—19.

47. Hart, "Letter to Elizabeth Lynch," p. 2.

48. Horsford, *A Voice*, pp. 214–15. The date of Elizabeth Thwaites's death is also recorded in Horsford, p. 213.

49. Findlay and Holdsworth, *Wesleyan Methodist Missionary Society*, p. 140.

50. Horsford, *A Voice*, p. 211. Note also that Joseph Phillips refused to release certain papers to the committee and was sent to jail for about a year. Among British Evangelicals he became a cause célèbre. This same Joseph Phillips would later testify on behalf of Mary Prince, the ex-slave whose memoirs caused an uproar in Britain in 1831.

51. Horsford, *A Voice*, p. 212. The exact details of Elizabeth Hart Thwaites's testimony are unclear as records conflict somewhat. Aside from Horsford's record, which insists that she "held out" and kept silence, there is commentary in Charles Thwaites's journal that suggests she concurred because she did not think her answers would harm people. See Charles Thwaites's journal, no. 1, pp. 1–3. The holograph of this journal is in the Methodist Missionary Archives, London. For a full text of the journal entry, see Ferguson, ed., *The Hart Sisters*.

52. Macqueen, "The Colonial Empire of Great Britain," *Blackwoods Magazine* (November 1832): 744–64.

53. Goveia, *Slave Society*, p. 218. For a discussion of free people of color in San Domingan society, see David Patrick Geggus, *Slavery, War, and Revolution. The British Occupation of Saint Domingue 1793–1798.* (Oxford: Clarendon

Press, 1982), pp. 18–23 and passim. As emancipation became a reality, the matter became even more heated. Note, too, that the matter of discrimination against free people of color reached such a point of acrimony that in 1823 members of the community presented a petition of their grievances.

54. F. K. Prochaska, *Women and Philanthropy in Nineteenth-Century England* (Oxford: Clarendon Press, 1980), pp. 8–10, 99–100.

55. Lanaghan, *Antigua and the Antiguans,* 1: 99.

56. The Reverend Thomas Coke quoted in Gilbert, *History of Methodism,* p. 17. The Reverend Thomas Coke is initially very favorably disposed toward the revolution in San Domingo. See Coke, *A History of the West Indies,* especially pp. 432–530. Later, however, he seems to have prevaricated. His vacillation may help to explain the spiritual but not the political aspect of the Hart sisters' conflict.

57. Goveia, *Slave Society,* p. 295.

58. Said, *Orientalism.* See particularly the introduction for Said's argument about the production of knowledge and the representation of (often subject) peoples in the interests of the colonial ruling class. Said argues that one group, usually dominant, distance or offensively represent another group, usually thought of as subjugated or the "other."

59. Mohanty, "Drawing the Color Line," in *The Bounds of Race: Perspectives on Hegemony and Resistance,* edited and introduced by LaCapra, p. 313.

60. Morrison, *Playing in the Dark,* p. 45.

61. Foucault, *Power/Knowledge,* pp. 100–102.

62. Fanon, *Black Skin, White Masks,* especially ch. 4. See also Frantz Fanon, *The Wretched of the Earth* (New York: Grove, 1963), p. 49 and passim.

4. Mansfield Park: *Plantocratic Paradigms*

1. Sypher, "The West-Indian," pp. 504–5, 509.

2. Morrison, *Playing in the Dark,* pp. 44–45.

3. Craton, *Testing the Chains.*

4. Goveia, *Slave Society.* See also D. J. Murray, *The West Indies and the Development of Colonial Government 1801——1834.* (Oxford: Clarendon Press, 1965); Dale Herbert Porter, *The Defense of the British Slave Trade, 1784–1807.* (doctoral dissertation, University of Oregon, 1967, pp. 25–166.

5. Mary Millard points out that Northampton squires rarely were sugar planters and speculates that "an earlier Bertram married a lady who brought an estate in Antigua, as her dowry." Mary Millard, "1807 and All That," *Persuasions* 8 (December 16, 1986): 50–51. I thank Kenneth Moler for invaluable discussions on the question of Sir Thomas's slave-owning status.

6. Sir Thomas probably belonged to the outer ring of absentee planters and merchants who had never visited the colonies. Between 1807 and 1833 forty-nine planters and twenty merchants belonged to this group. B. W. Higman,

4. Mansfield Park: *Plantocratic Paradigms*

"The West India 'Interest' in Parliament 1807–1833," *Historical Studies* 13 (October 1967–April 1969) 4: 1–19. See also Ragatz, *Absentee Landlordism*, pp. 1–19).

7. R. Williams, *The Country and the City*, pp. 279–80.

8. Stephen, *Anti-Slavery Recollections*, pp. 36–37. Note also that as a result of information about ongoing inhumane treatment, British abolitionists were shortly to publicize the condition of slaves in Antigua even more decisively in forming a committee for the "Neglected and Deserted Negroes" of that island. See John Rylands Memorial Library, Manchester, England, "The Case of the Neglected and Deserted Negroes in the Island of Antigua," anonymous pamphlet 21.5, pt. 8.

9. Klingberg, *The Anti-Slavery Movement in England*, pp. 131, 171–72. B. W. Higman, *Slave Populations*. See also James Walvin, "The Rise of British Popular Sentiment for Abolition, 1787–1832," in Bolt and Drescher, eds., *Anti-Slavery, Religion, and Reform*, p. 154 and passim; Stephen, *Anti-Slavery Recollections*, pp. 25–27 and passim.

10. Fleishman, *A Reading of Mansfield Park*, pp. 40–42.

11. Ibid., pp. 35–36.

12. Chapman, *The Novels of Jane Austen*, 3: 30. The enormous chain of expenses that emanated from the Great House included a host of people from servants and overseers to waiters, "brownskin gals" with no official function, and the estate's managing attorney who received 60 percent of the gross (Craton, *Sinews of Empire*, pp. 132–39).

13. Fleishman, *A Reading of Mansfield Park*, p. 37.

14. Willcox touches briefly on the turmoil that would have precipitated Sir Thomas's decision, in *Age of Aristocracy*, pp. 174–79. Willcox also points out that "though Miss Austen's two brothers were in the navy throughout the war, her world is untouched by anything outside itself; it is tranquil and timeless" (p. 168). See also Austen, *Mansfield Park*, p. 65.

15. Austen, *Mansfield Park*, p. 178.

16. With respect to Sir Thomas's near-noble status, Fleishman argues in *A Reading of Mansfield Park* that "only some four hundred families could qualify for the higher class, and despite an economic fluidity which enabled some baronets and even commoners to enter it, this was an aristocracy composed mainly of noblemen" (p. 40). Lanaghan, *Antigua and the Antiguans*, 2: 136.

17. Stephen, *Anti-Slavery Recollections*, pp. 8–19; Klingberg, *The Anti-Slavery Movement in England*, pp. 176–81.

18. Austen, *Mansfield Park*, p. 26.

19. Chapman, *The Novels of Jane Austen*, pp. 553–56.

20. Frank Gibbon, "The Antiguan Connection: Some New Light on *Mansfield Park*," in *Cambridge Quarterly*, 11 (1982): 303.

21. Clarkson, *African Slave-Trade*, 1: 378ff, 477ff. In reading Clarkson, Jane Austen would have been abreast of fierce abolitionist and proslavery infighting

both inside and outside Parliament and of the literature on the subject of the slave trade.

22. Ibid., 1: 479.

23. Austen, *Mansfield Park*, p. 370.

24. Hart, "Letter . . . to a Friend," in Horsford, *A Voice*, p. 11.

25. Austen, *Mansfield Park*, pp. 10–11.

26. Ibid., p. 18.

27. Ibid., p. 11.

28. Johanna M. Smith, "My Only Sister Now: Incest in *Mansfield Park*," *Studies in the Novel* 19 (Spring 1987)1: 1–15.

29. Yeazell, "The Boundaries of *Mansfield Park*," pp. 133–52. Although Jane Austen despised Methodism, some evangelical thinking on the part of Fanny Price does underpin *Mansfield Park*. Fanny Price, for example, despises the wantonness of the Crawfords' lives and the degeneracy associated with play-acting. At some level—though the point is certainly arguable—she enacts the "Good life—visibly Christian, humble, contemplative, serviceable," Butler, *Jane Austen and the War of Ideas*, p. 243. Fanny Price does not demur at dancing, however, as Elizabeth Hart Thwaites does.

30. Austen, *Mansfield Park*, pp. 26–27.

31. Ibid., p. 318.

32. Todorov, *The Conquest of America*, p. 130.

33. Austen, *Mansfield Park*, pp. 388, 390.

34. Ibid., p. 377.

35. For example, in *Popular Tales* (1804), Maria Edgeworth has a story entitled "The Grateful Negro," which exemplifies this familiar binary opposition. It is possible, given Jane Austen's admiration for Maria Edgeworth (Chapman, *The Novels of Jane Austen*, 5: 299), that she had read some of Edgeworth's tales as well as her words. Given the popularity of *The Farmer of Inglewood Forest* by Elizabeth Helme, which also features a "grateful Negro," Austen may well have read that novel or others featuring that motif. Note here, too, that Fanny Price acts as a good evangelical in abhorring private theatricals. At some level she would concur ideologically with the Hart sisters, although Elizabeth Hart Thwaites was stricter. See Butler, *Jane Austen*, p. 231.

36. Austen, *Mansfield Park*, p. 217. The connection of indolent house-mistresses despised by their authors frequently appears. Two examples are Lady Ellison in Sarah Robinson Scott's novel, *The History of George Ellison* (London: Millar, 1766), and Mary Wollstonecraft's polemical attack on such practices in *The Rights of Woman* (1792).

37. Austen, *Mansfield Park*, p. 196.

38. Sypher, "The West-Indian," pp. 503, 506.

39. Ragatz, *Absentee Lordlordism*, pp. 1–21. Note also how Sir Thomas's "burnt, fagged, worn look" (*Mansfield Park*, p. 178) matches signs of the

contemporary West Indian in fiction: "A yellowish complexion, lassitude of body and mind, fitful spells of passion or energy, generosity bordering on improvidence, sentimentality combined with a streak of haughtiness and cruelty to subordinates" (Sypher, "The West-Indian," p. 504).

40. Kotzebue, *Lovers' Vows*. . . ., translated by Mrs. Inchbald (London: G. G. and J. Robinson, 1798) in Chapman, *The Novels of Jane Austen*, pp. 475–538.

41. Kotzebue, *Lovers' Vows*, p. 534. Philosophically anti-Jacobin, Kotzebue champions ideas of a basically benevolent human nature (Butler, p. 234; Kirkham, pp. 93–97, 100–116). Note also that Jane Austen expects that audiences will have an overall sense both of the contemporary debate over the immorality of play-acting and of the play's philosophical, pro-Jacobin underpinnings (Butler, *Jane Austen and the War of Ideas*, pp. 231, 234).

42. Gibbon, "The Antiguan Connection," pp. 298–305 and pp. 304–5.

43. Gerald L. Gould, "The Gate Scene at Sotherton in *Mansfield Park*," in *Literature and Psychology* 20 (1970) 1: 75–78.

44. For the discussions of subjectivity and interpellation in ideology here and elsewhere in the essay, I am indebted to Pêcheux, *Language, Semantics, and Ideology*.

45. I am assuming here and elsewhere in the text the reader's conversancy with *Lovers' Vows*, an assumption I think Jane Austen makes.

46. Butler, *Jane Austen and the War of Ideas*, p. 93.

47. In *Discipline and Punish*, Foucault argues that feudal torture of the criminal's body and subsequent death "made everyone aware . . . of the unrestrained presence [and power] of the sovereign . . . . The ceremony of the public torture and execution displayed for all to see the power relation that gave his force to the law. . . .We must regard the public execution, as it was still ritualized in the eighteenth century, as a political operation" (pp. 49–53).

48. Jane Austen, *Emma*, first published in 1816 by Houghton Mifflin (Boston: Riverside Press, 1933), p. 233.

49. Ibid., p. 233.

50. Kirkham, *Jane Austen*, p. 132.

51. See Shyllon, *Black Slaves in Britain*, especially pp. 77–124 and pp. 237–43. See also Walvin, *The Black Presence*, pp. 95–114.

52. Kirkham, *Jane Austen*, pp. 116–19. I thank Terry Castle for first pointing out the resonance of emancipation.

53. Austen, *Mansfield Park*, p. 472.

54. For the argument about the text's excess, I am indebted to Macherey's *Theory of Literary Production*, pp. 75–97 and passim.

55. Austen, *Mansfield Park*, p. 526.

56. Yeazel, "The Boundaries of *Mansfield Park*," p. 133.

57. Austen, *Mansfield Park*, p. 198.

58. Craton, *Testing the Chains*, pp. 337–38.

59. Austen, *Mansfield Park*, p. 104. I would add data from the *Quarterly Review* of 1811 to Chapman's list of sources for *Mansfield Park* and refashion his chronology of the novel from 1800–1809 accordingly.

60. See Gilbert Mathison, *Quarterly Review*, article 9, "Notices respecting Jamaica, in 1808, 1809, 1810" (1811), 6: 164.

61. Pêcheux, *Language, Semantics, and Ideology*, p. 13.

62. I am thinking here of Said's conceptualization of orientalizing in ch. 1, "The Scope of Orientalism," and passim in *Orientalism*.

63. Pêcheux, *Language, Semantics, and Ideology*, pp. 156, 157.

5. Sending the Younger Son Across the Wide Sargasso Sea: The New Colonizer Arrives

1. Jean Rhys, *Wide Sargasso Sea* (1966; reprint New York: W. W. Norton, 1982), p. 17. All references will be to the Norton edition. For details of Jean Rhys's upbringing in Dominica, see particularly Jean Rhys, *Smile Please*, pp. 13–76. See also Dance, ed. *Fifty Caribbean Writers*, especially pp. 390–401.

2. See S. James, *The Ladies and the Mammies*. For details of Dominican emigration, see Myers, *Dominica*, pp. xvii–xxi.

3. Note also Jean Rhys's comments on *Jane Eyre* as she composes *Wide Sargasso Sea* and transforms Bertha: "Finally I got Jane Eyre to read and reread and hook on my Mrs Rochester to Charlotte Brontë's. I was a bit taken aback when I discovered what a fat (and improbable) monster she was. However I think I have seen how to do it though not without pain struggle curses and lamentation. (Whether I have any *right* to do it is a question which I'll face later. One thing at a time.)" (Wyndham and Melly, eds., *Jean Rhys Letters, 1931–1966*, p. 149).

4. Cudjoe, ed., *Caribbean Women Writers*, p. 113. For a compelling reading of the role of the mother in Rhys's "invention" of a "history for Bertha Mason," see Kloepfer, *The Unspeakable Mother*, especially p. 142ff.

5. Ramchand, *The West Indian Novel*, p. 234.

6. Rubin, "The Traffic in Women," pp. 157–210. See also Nebeker, *Jean Rhys*, especially pp. 124–25.

7. For an inspired reading of *Robinson Crusoe*, see Hulme, *Colonial Encounters*, especially pp. 175–224.

8. Hall, *A Brief History of the West India Committee*, pp. 86–88.

9. Green, *British Slave Emancipation*, p. 221.

10. Ibid., p. 235.

11. Ibid., p. 238.

12. Davy, *The West Indies*, p. 504.

13. Ibid., pp. 504–5.

14. Jean Rhys's early autobiography is full of allusions to her gradual with-

drawal from family and community as she came to terms with her society as she grew up. (*Smile Please*, pp. 46, 50, and passim.) At one point she talks of the "identification or annihilation I longed for" (p. 67).

15. Note that Jean Rhys discusses cockroaches at length in her autobiography. Growing up she hated them because of what she was told about them by Meta, a black servant. The metonymic transformation in *Wide Sargasso Sea* is very pointed. Now she is and symbolizes the cockroach in the African-Caribbean community. Rhys discusses mashed centipedes as part of the same scenario between her and Meta. See *Smile Please*, p. 23.

16. Honeychurch, *Dominica: A History of an Island*, p. 44.

17. Curiously enough, Jean Rhys explains in her autobiography that "we believed, or I believed, that Diablotin was eight thousand feet high and that it had never been climbed because the summit was rock. Round it flew large black birds called Diablotins (devil birds), found nowhere else in the West Indies or the world" (*Smile Please*, p. 15). In *Wide Sargasso Sea* her description of Christophine as a black devil intertextualizes not only an awe of Christophine but a sense of Christophine as a unique person.

18. Thomas Atwood describes the tradition and practices of obeah in Dominica, to which Christophine is heir, from an eighteenth-century ethnocentric historian's viewpoint (Atwood, *The History of the Island of Dominica*, pp. 268–74). For Rhys's ethnocentrisms, see also Plante, *Difficult Women*, p. 42.

19. Chatoyer, "The Declaration of Joseph Chatoyer, Chief of the Chariabs," in *An Account of the Black Chariabs*, pp. 117–18. See also Craton, *Testing the Chains*, pp. 149–53.

20. For an autobiographical dimension where Rhys discusses a maid called Josephine, see *Smile Please*, p. 38. See also Knapton, *Empress Josephine*.

21. Marks and de Courtivron, eds., *New French Feminisms: An Anthology*, pp. 258–59.

22. For an account of mimicking that pertains here, see Fanon, *Black Skin, White Masks*, ch. 1.

23. Sandler with Freud, *The Analysis of Defense*, p. 437. For Rochester's loathing of the idea she could be free, see Tiffin, "Mirror and Mask," pp. 328–41.

24. Said, *Orientalism*, pp. 21 and 31.

25. I am indebted here to Macherey's explication of this idea in *A Theory of Literary Production*, pp. 150, 194–99.

26. Spivak, "Three Women's Texts," p. 272.

27. Certainly even in retropect Rhys seems unable in *Smile Please* to compute Meta's actions as sabotage or perverse opposition to the dominant order.

28. Rhys, *Smile Please*, p. 51.

29. *The New Encyclopaedia Britannica* (Chicago: Encyclopaedia Britannica, 1991) 10: 452.

30. For elaborations on the sea, see also S. James, *The Ladies and the Mammies*, p. 62. Note also Rhys's description of the sea toward the end of the section on Dominica in her autobiography: "the blue, the treacherous tremendous sea" (*Smile Please*, p. 71).

31. S. James, *The Ladies and the Mammies*, pp. 68–72.

32. S. James usefully summarizes the controversy over the jump to Tia in *The Ladies and the Mammies*, pp. 90–92.

33. Ibid., pp. 72–73.

34. Spivak, "Three Women's Texts," p. 269.

6. A Small Place: *Glossing Annie John's Rebellion*

1. Jamaica Kincaid, *Annie John* (New York: New American Library, 1983), p. 29. All references are to this edition.

2. Jamaica Kincaid, *A Small Place* (London: Virago, 1988). All references are to this edition.

3. Cudjoe, ed., *Caribbean Women Writers*, p. 220.

4. For concentrated biographical information on Jamaica Kincaid, see particularly Cudjoe, ed., *Caribbean Women Writers*, pp. 215–32, and Dance, ed., *Fifty Caribbean Writers*, pp. 255–63. See also Garis, "Through West Indian Eyes."

5. Sigmund Freud discusses the relationship between water and pre-oedipal harmony (*The Interpretation of Dreams*, pp. 434–37).

6. Cixous, "The Laugh of the Medusa," p. 251.

7. For issues of projection and displacement, see Anna Freud, *Ego*, vol. 2, especially ch. 5.

8. This information comes directly from Jamaica Kincaid, who talks about her life in several interviews. See, for example, Perry, "An Interview with Jamaica Kincaid," and Cudjoe, ed., *Caribbean Women Writers*, p. 220 and passim.

9. Sandra Gilbert and Susan Gubar, *The Madwoman in the Attic: Women Writers and the Literary Imagination* (New Haven: Yale University Press, 1979), p. 269.

10. See, for example, Marilyn Lawrence, *The Anorexic Experience* (London: Women's Press, 1984), pp. 32–39 and passim; Suzanne Abraham and Derek Llewellyn-Jones, *Eating Disorders: The Facts* (Oxford University Press, 1984); and Felicia Romeo, *Understanding Anorexia Nervosa* (Springfield, Ill.: Charles Thomas, 1986).

11. See Cora Kaplan, "Language and Gender," in *Sea Changes: Essays on Culture and Feminism* (London: Verso, 1986), especially pp. 78–80.

12. See Averil Mackenzie-Grieve, *The Last Years of the English Slave Trade, Liverpool, 1750–1807* (New York: Cass, 1968), p. 156. For obeah, see also

Goveia, *Slave Society*, pp. 245–47, and Cudjoe, ed., *Caribbean Women Writers*, pp. 225–31. The telling phrase comes from Carole Boyce Davies, "Writing Home," p. 65.

13. For the discussion of Annie John's conditioning, her construction of subjectivity, see Louis Althusser, "Ideology and Ideological State Apparatuses," in *Lenin and Other Essays* (New York: Monthly Review, 1970), pp. 127–86.

14. It is conceivable that Jamaica Kincaid is referring to an abridged version of Bryan Edwards's notoriously racist text, *The History, Civil and Commercial of the British Colonies in the West Indies*, 2 vols. (London, 1793). Edwards was a well-known planter and English politician.

15. Todorov talks extensively about Columbus as the signifier of colonial power and the anxieties of the colonizer in *The Conquest of America*, especially pp. 3–50.

16. In a reading at the University of Nebraska at Lincoln, November 9, 1990, Marlene Nourbese Philip stated that "playing around with fiction and fact is a black thing."

17. Valerie Smith in "Black Feminist Theory and the Representation of the 'Other' " in Cheryl Wall, ed., *Changing Our Own Words: Essays on Criticism, Theory, and Writing by Black Women* (New Brunswick, N.J.: Rutgers University Press, 1989), p. 55.

18. James, *The Ladies and the Mammies*.

19. *Paradise Lost* is a clever choice on several fronts. Apart from the references to Milton and the implications of the British literary canon, *paradise* could also refer to Columbus's "most striking" belief in the earthly paradise. He is looking for this place when he stumbles on the Caribbean (Todorov, *The Conquest of America*, pp. 16–18).

20. Cudjoe, ed., *Caribbean Women Writers*, p. 218.

21. Enid Blyton, *Here Comes Noddy* (London: Sampson Low, Marston and Richards Press, 1951).

22. Bob Dixon, *Catching Them Young: Sex, Race, and Class in Children's Fiction—Political Ideas in Children's Fiction* (London: Pluto, 1977), 2: 56–73. For *Here Comes Noddy*, see particularly Sheila G. Ray, *The Blyton Phenomenon: The Controversy Surrounding the World's Most Successful Children's Writer* (London: Andre Deutsch, 1982), p. 104.

23. Garis, "Through West Indian Eyes," pp. 42–44, 70–91.

24. For my discussion in this section, I am indebted to Gayatri Chakravorty Spivak's discussions in "Draupadi," in *In Other Worlds: Essays on Cultural Politics* (New York: Methuen, 1987), pp. 179–87, and in "Three Women's Texts and a Critique of Imperialism," in *The Feminist Reader: Essays on Gender and the Politics of Literary Criticism*, edited by Catherine Belsey and Jane Moore (New York: Basil Blackwell, 1989), p. 175–95.

25. For an elaboration of this point, see Mary Jacobus, "A Difference of

7. Conclusion

View," in Mary Jacobus, ed., *Women Writers and Writing About Women* (New York: Barnes and Noble Imports, 1979), pp. 10–21. For a valuable discussion of textuality, see Elizabeth Meese, *Crossing the Double Cross: The Practice of Feminist Criticism* (Chapel Hill: University of North Caroline Press, 1986), p. 44.

26. Spivak, "Three Women's texts," p. 187.

27. Barbara Christian, "But What Do We Think We're Doing Anyway: The State of Black Feminist Criticism(s) or My Version of a Little Bit of History," in Wall, ed., *Changing Our Own Words*, p. 73.

28. Spivak, "Three Women's Texts," p. 187.

29. Kincaid, *A Small Place*, p. 30.

30. Said, *Orientalism*, p. 20.

31. Audre Lorde, "Eye to Eye," in *Sister Outsider* (Tramansburg, N.Y.: Crossing Press, 1984), p. 147.

32. In his analysis of Sahagun, Todorov underlines the anxieties generated in imperialists by the fear of the colonized peoples' literacy, *The Conquest of America*, p. 221 and passim. In a slightly different context, Henry Louis Gates, Jr., evaluates the crucial roles of literacy among slaves in *Figures in Black: Words, Signs and the Racial Self* (London: Oxford University Press, 1987).

33. Marlene Nourbese Philips's poem entitled "Discourse on the Logic of Language," in Nasta, ed., *Motherlands*.

34. Goveia, *Slave Society*, pp. 134–36, 156–57, and passim.

35. Donna Perry, "Initiation in Jamaica Kincaid's *Annie John*," in Cudjoe, ed., *Caribbean Women Writers*, p. 253.

36. This argument borrows from Jacques Lacan's ideas about psychosexual development in Jacques Lacan, *Écrits: A Selection*, translated by Alan Sheridan (London: Tavistock, 1977), especially pp. 1–7.

7. Conclusion

1. In *Feminism Without Illusions*, Elizabeth Fox-Genovese presents contradictions in Mary Wollstonecraft's exhortation and argues that these very demands for individual rights (as opposed, say, to a collectively waged struggle) are a political trap, a dead end, Elizabeth Fox-Genovese, *Feminism Without Illusions. A Critique of Individualism* (Chapel Hill and London: University of North Carolina Press, 1991), pp. 1–10 and passim.

2. Chandra Talpade Mohanty, "Under Western Eyes: Feminist Scholarship and Colonial Discourses," in *Third World Women and the Politics of Feminism*, edited by Chandra Talpade Mohanty, Ann Russo, and Lourdes Torres (Bloomington and Indianapolis: Indiana University Press, 1991), p. 53.

Selective Bibliography

Manuscript Sources

Gilbert, Anne Hart. A *History of Methodism*. School of Oriental and African Studies, University of London, Methodist Missionary Correspondence.

Thwaites, Elizabeth Hart. A *History of Methodism*. School of Oriental and African Studies, University of London, Methodist Missionary Correspondence.

Thwaites, Charles. *Journal and Correspondence*. School of Oriental and African Studies, University of London, Methodist Missionary Correspondence.

Books and Articles

Ashcroft, Bill, Gareth Griffiths, and Helen Tiffin. *The Empire Writes Back: Theory and Practice in Post-Colonial Literatures*. London: Routledge, 1989.

Atwood, Thomas. *The History of the Island of Dominica*. . . . 1791. Reprint. London: Cass, 1971.

Austen, Jane. *Mansfield Park*. 1814. Reprint, Middlesex, England: Penguin, 1966.

———. *Emma*. 1816. Boston: Riverside Press, 1933.

Barlow, Joel. *Advice to the Privileged Orders in the Several States of Europe*. Ithaca, N.Y.: Great Seal, 1956.

Bolt, Christine and Seymour Drescher, eds. *Anti-Slavery, Religion, and Reform:*

Bibliography

Essays in Memory of Roger Anstey. Kent, England: Archon Books, Dawson, 1980.

Box, Reverend William. *Memoir of John Gilbert, Esq., Late Naval Storekeeper at Antigua . . . .* Liverpool: Marples, 1835.

Braithwaite, Edward. *The Development of Creole Society in Jamaica, 1770–1820*. Oxford: Clarendon Press, 1971.

Bush, Barbara. *Slave Women in Caribbean Society, 1650–1838*. Bloomington: Indiana University Press, 1990.

Butler, Marilyn. *Jane Austen and the War of Ideas*. Oxford: Clarendon Press, 1975.

Chapman, R. W. *The Novels of Jane Austen: The Text Based on Collation of the Early Editions*. 5 vols. London: Oxford University Press, 1923.

Chatoyer, Joseph. "The Delaration of Joseph Chatoyer, Chief of the Chariabs." In *An Account of the Black Chariabs in the Island of St. Vincents . . . Compiled from the Papers of the Late Sir William Young*. London: Sewell, 1795.

Chatterjee, Partha. *Nationalist Thought and the Colonial World: A Derivative Discourse?* Tokyo: Zed Books, United Nations University, 1986.

Cixous, Hélène. "The Laugh of the Medusa." In *New French Feminisms: An Anthology*, edited by Elaine Marks and Isabelle de Courtivron. New York: Schocken, 1981.

Clarkson, Thomas. *The History of the Rise, Progress, and Accomplishment of the Abolition of the African Slave-Trade by the British Parliament*. 2 vols. 1808. Reprint, London: Cass, 1968.

Coke, Thomas. *A History of the West Indies . . . .* London: Blanshard, 1811.

Coupland, Sir Reginald. *The British Anti-Slavery Movement*. London: Cass, 1933.

——. *The Exploitation of East Africa, 1856–1890: The Slave Trade and the Scramble*. Chicago: Northwestern University Press, 1967.

Cracknell, Basil E. *Dominica*. Harrisburg, Pa.: David & Charles, Newton Abbot Stackpole Books, 1973.

Craton, Michael. *Sinews of Empire: A Short History of British Slavery*. Garden City, N.Y.: Anchor/Doubleday, 1974.

——. *Testing the Chains: Resistance to Slavery in the British West Indies*. Ithaca: Cornell University Press, 1982.

Craton, Michael and James Walvin. *A Jamaican Plantation: The History of Worthy Park, 1670–1970*. Toronto: University of Toronto, 1970.

Craton, Michael, James Walvin, and David Wright. *Slavery, Abolition, and Emancipation: Black Slaves and the British Empire*. London: Longman, 1976.

Cudjoe, Selwyn R., ed. *Caribbean Women Writers: Essays from the First International Conference*. Wellesley, Mass.: Calaloux, 1990.

Dance, Daryl Cumber, ed. *Fifty Caribbean Writers: A Bio-Bibliographical Critical Sourcebook*. New York: Greenwood, 1986.

Davidson, Arnold E. *Jean Rhys*. New York: Frederick Ungar, 1985.

Davies, Carole Boyce. "Writing Home: Gender and Heritage in the Works of Afro-Caribbean/American Women Writers." *Out of the Kumbla: Caribbean Women and Literature*, edited by Carole Boyce Davies and Elaine Savory Fido. Trenton, N.J.: Africa World Press, 1990.

Davis, Kortright. *Emancipation Still Comin': Explorations in Caribbean Emancipatory Theology*. Maryknoll, N.Y.: Orbis, 1990.

Davy, John. *The West Indies Before and Since Slave Emancipation* . . . . 1854. Reprint, London: Cass, 1971.

Drescher, Seymour. *Capitalism and Antislavery: British Mobilization in Comparative Perspective*. London: Macmillan, 1986.

Edwards, Paul, ed. *Equiano's Travels: His Autobiography—The Interesting Narrative of the Life of Olaudah Equiano or Gustavus Vassa the African*. London: Heinemann, 1967.

Estwick, Samuel. *Considerations of the Negro Cause Commonly So Called*. London: Dodsley, 1788.

Fanon, Frantz. *Black Skin, White Masks*. New York: Grove, 1967; London: Pluto, 1986.

Ferguson, Moira. *First Feminists: British Women Writers, 1578–1799*. Bloomington: Indiana University Press, 1985.

———. *The History of Mary Prince: A West Indian Slave, Related by Herself*. London: Pandora, 1987.

———. *Subject to Others: British Women Writers and Colonial Slavery, 1670–1834*. New York and London: Routledge, Chapman and Hall, 1992.

———, ed. *The Hart Sisters: Early African Caribbean Writers, Evangelicals, and Radicals*. Lincoln: *University of Nebraska Press, 1993*.

Findlay, G. G. and W. W. Holdsworth. *The History of the Wesleyan Methodist Missionary Society*. 5 vols. London: Epworth, 1921.

Fleishman, Avrom. *A Reading of Mansfield Park: An Essay in Critical Synthesis*. Minneapolis: University of Minnesota Press, 1967.

Flexner, Eleanor. *Mary Wollstonecraft: A Biography*. New York: Coward, McCann & Geoghegan, 1972.

Foucault, Michel. *Power/Knowledge: Selected Interviews and Other Writings, 1972–1977*. Edited by Colin Gordon and translated by Colin Gordon, Leo Marshall, John Mepham, and Kate Soper. New York: Pantheon, 1972.

———. *Discipline and Punish: The Birth of the Prison*. New York: Vintage House, 1979.

Fox-Genovese, Elizabeth. *Feminism Without Illusions: A Critique of Individualism*. Chapel Hill: University of North Carolina Press, 1991.

Freud, Anna. *The Ego and the Mechanisms of Defense: The Writings of Anna Freud*. 2 vols. Translated by Cecil Baines. Vol. 2. New York: International University Press, 1966.

Freud, Sigmund. *An Outline of Psycho-Analysis*. New York: Norton, 1949.

——. *The Interpretation of Dreams*. Translated and edited by James Strachey. New York: Discus, 1965.

Garis, Leslie. "Through West Indian Eyes." *New York Times Magazine*, October 19, 1990, pp. 42–44 and passim.

Gasper, David Barry. *Bondmen and Rebels: A Study of Master-Slave Relations in Antigua, with Implications for Colonial British America*. Baltimore: Johns Hopkins University Press, 1985.

Gates, Henry, Louis, ed. *"Race," Writing, and Difference*. Chicago: University of Chicago Press, 1985.

——, ed. *Reading Black, Reading Feminist: A Critical Anthology*. New York: Penguin, 1990.

Geggus, David Patrick. *Slavery, War, and Revolution: The British Occupation of Saint Dominique, 1793—1798*. Oxford: Clarendon Press, 1982.

Gibbon, Frank. "The Antiguan Connection: Some New Light on *Mansfield Park*." *Cambridge Quarterly* 15 (1982): 303.

Goveia, Elsa V. *Slave Society in the British Leeward Islands at the End of the Eighteenth Century*. New Haven: Yale University Press, 1965.

Green, William A. *British Slave Emancipation: The Sugar Colonies and the Great Experiment, 1830–1865*. Oxford: Clarendon Press, 1976.

Grieve, Symington. *Notes Upon the Island of Dominica . . . .* London: Adam & Charles Black, 1906.

Hall, Douglas. *A Brief History of the West India Committee*. Barbados: Caribbean Universities Press, 1971.

Hart, Elizabeth, "Letter from Miss Elizabeth Hart to a Friend." 1794. In John Horsford, *A Voice from the West Indies . . . .* London: Heylin, 1856.

Hays, Mary. *Memoirs of Emma Courtney*. 2 vols. New York: Garland, 1974.

Helme, Elizabeth. *The Farmer of Inglewood Forest*. London: Minerva Press, 1796.

Higman, B. W. *Slave Populations of the British Caribbean, 1807–1834*. Baltimore: Johns Hopkins University Press, 1984.

Honeychurch, Lennox. *The Dominica Story: A History of the Island*. Lennox Honeychurch, 1975.

Horsford, John. *A Voice from the West Indies . . . .* London: Heylin, 1856.

Hulme, Peter. *Colonial Encounters: Europe and the Native Caribbean, 1492–1797*. London and New York: Methuen, 1986.

Iser, Wolfgang. *The Implied Reader: Patterns of Communications in Prose Fiction from Bunyan to Beckett*. Baltimore: Johns Hopkins University Press, 1974.

James, C. L. R. *The Black Jacobins: Toussaint L'Ouverture and the San Domingo Revolution*. 2d ed., rev. New York: Random House, 1963.

——. "The Making of the Caribbean People." In *At the Rendezvous of Victory: Selected Writings*. London: Allison & Busby, 1984.

165

James, Selma. *The Ladies and the Mammies: Jane Austen and Jean Rhys.* Bristol: British Falling Wall Press, 1983.

Jordan, Winthrop D. *White Over Black: American Attitudes Toward the Negro, 1550–1812.* Chapel Hill: University of North Carolina Press, 1968.

Kamuf, Peggy. *Fictions of Feminine Desire.* Lincoln: University of Nebraska Press, 1982.

Katrak, Ketu H. "Decolonizing Culture: Toward a Theory for Postcolonial Women's Texts." *Modern Fiction Studies* 35, no. 1 (1989): 157–79.

Keener, Frederick M. and Susan E. Lorsch, eds. *Eighteenth-Century Women and the Arts.* New York: Greenwood, 1988.

Kincaid, Jamaica. *Annie John.* New York: New American Library, 1983. All references are to this edition.

——. *A Small Place.* London: Virago, 1988. All references are to this edition.

Kirkham, Margaret. *Jane Austen: Feminism and Fiction.* New York: Methuen, 1986.

Klingberg, Frank Joseph. *The Anti-Slavery Movement in England: A Study in English Humanitarianism.* New Haven: Yale University Press, 1926.

Kloepfer, Deborah Kelly. *The Unspeakable Mother: Forbidden Discourse in Jean Rhys and H.D..* Ithaca: Cornell University Press, 1989.

Knapton, Ernest John. *Empress Josephine.* Cambridge, Mass.: Harvard University Press, 1964.

Lanaghan, Frances. *Antigua and the Antiguans . . . .* 2 vols. London: Saunders and Otley, 1844.

MacDowell, Douglas. *Spartan Law.* Edinburgh: Scottish Academic Press, 1986.

Macherey, Pierre. *A Theory of Literary Production.* Translated by Geoffrey Wall. London: Routledge & Kegan Paul, 1978.

McKeon, Michael. *The Origins of the English Novel, 1600–1940.* Baltimore: Johns Hopkins University Press, 1987.

Macqueen, James. "The Colonial Empire of Great Britain." *Blackwoods Magazine* (November 1832): 744–64.

Mannoni, O. *Prospero and Caliban: The Psychology of Colonization.* Translated by Pamela Powesland. New York: Praeger, 1964.

Marks, Elaine and Isabelle de Courtivron, eds. *New French Feminisms: An Anthology.* New York: Schocken, 1981.

Marshall, Madeleine Forell and Janet Todd. *English Congregational Hymns in the Eighteenth Century.* Lexington: University of Kentucky Press, 1982.

Mathieson, William Law. *British Slavery and Its Abolition, 1823–1838.* New York: Octagon, 1967.

Michell, H. *Sparta.* Cambridge: Cambridge University Press, 1952.

Millard, Mary. "1807 and All That." *Persuasions* 8 (December 16, 1986): 50–51.

Miller, Christopher. *Blank Darkness: Africanist Discourse in English.* Chicago: University of Chicago Press, 1985.

Miner, Earl, ed. *Stuart and Georgian Moments: Clark Library Seminar Papers on Seventeenth- and Eighteenth-Century English Literature*. Berkeley: University of California Press, 1972.

Mohanty, Chandra Talpade, Ann Russo, and Lourdes Torres, eds. *Third World Women and the Politics of Feminism*. Bloomington: Indiana University Press, 1991.

Mohanty, Satya P. "Drawing the Color Line: Kipling and the Culture of Colonial Rule." In *The Bounds of Race: Perspectives on Hegemony and Resistance*, edited and introduced by Dominick LaCapra. Ithaca: Cornell University Press, 1991.

More, Hannah. *The Works of Hannah More with a Story of Her Life*. 2 vols. Boston: Goodrich, 1927.

Morrison, Toni. *Playing in the Dark: Whiteness and the Literary Imagination*. Cambridge, Mass.: Harvard University Press, 1992.

Myers, Robert A. *Dominica*. Oxford: Clio, 1987.

Nasta, Susheila, ed. *Motherlands: Black Women's Writing from Africa, the Caribbean, and South Asia*. New Brunswick, N.J.: Rutgers University Press, 1991.

Nebeker, Helen. *Jean Rhys, Woman in Passage: A Critical Study of the Novels of Jean Rhys*. Montreal: Eden Press Women's Publications, 1981.

Nussbaum, Felicity A. *The Brink of All We Hate: English Satires on Women, 1660–1750*. Lexington: University of Kentucky Press, 1984.

———. *The Autobiographical Subject: Gender and Ideology in Eighteenth-Century English*. Baltimore: Johns Hopkins University Press, 1989.

O'Connor, Teresa F. *Jean Rhys: The West Indian Novels*. New York: New York University Press, 1986.

Parry, Benita. *Conrad and Imperialism: Ideological Boundaries and Visionary Frontiers*. London: Macmillan, 1983.

Pêcheux, Michel. *Language, Semantics, and Ideology*. New York: St. Martin's, 1975.

Perry, Donna. "An Interview with Jamaica Kincaid." In *Reading Black, Reading Feminist: A Critical Anthology*, edited by Henry Louis Gates, Jr. New York: Penguin, 1990.

Plante, David. *Difficult Women: A Memoir of Three*. New York: Dutton, 1979.

Ragatz, Lowell Joseph. *Absentee Landlordism in the British Caribbean, 1750–1833*. London: Bryan Edwards Press, n.d.

———. *A Guide for the Study of British Caribbean History, 1743–1834, Including the Abolition and Emancipation Movements*. Washington, D.C.: U.S. Government Printing Office, 1932.

Ramchand, Kenneth. *The West Indian Novel and Its Background*. New York: Barnes & Noble, 1970.

Rhys, Jean. *Smile Please: An Unfinished Autobiography*. New York: Harper & Row, 1979.

———. *Wide Sargasso Sea*. 1966. Reprint, New York: Norton, 1982.

Bibliography

Robinson, H. *Phillis Wheatley and Her Writings*. New York: Garland, 1984.

Rubin, Gayle. "The Traffic in Women: Notes on the 'Political Economy' of Sex." In *Toward an Anthropology of Women*, edited by Rayna R. Reitor. New York: Monthly Review Press, 1975.

Russell, G. W. E. *The Household of Faith*. London: Hodder and Stoughton, 1902.

Said, Edward W. *Orientalism*. New York: Vintage, 1979.

———. *The World, the Text, and the Critic*. Cambridge, Mass.: Harvard University Press, 1983.

Sandler, Joseph, with Anna Freud. *The Analysis of Defense: The Ego and the Mechanisms of Defense Revisited*. New York: International Universities Press, 1985.

Shimron, Benjamin. *Late Sparta: The Spartan Revolution, 243–146 B.C.* Arethusa Monographs III. Buffalo: Department of Classics, State University of New York, 1972.

Shyllon, F. O. *Black Slaves in Britain*. London: Oxford University Press, 1974.

Smith, Charlotte. *Desmond: A Novel*. 3 vols. New York: Garland, 1976.

Smith, Samuel Stanhope. 2d ed. 1810. Reissued as *An Essay on the Causes of the Variety of Complexion and Figure in the Human Species*, edited by Winthrop D. Jordan. Cambridge, Mass.: Harvard University Press, 1965.

Spacks, Patricia Meyer. "Early Fiction and the Frightened Male." *Novel* 8 (1974): 5–15.

Spivak, Gayatri Chakravorty. "Three Women's Texts and a Critique of Imperialism." In *"Race," Writing, and Difference*, edited by Henry Louis Gates, Jr. Chicago: University of Chicago Press, 1985.

Stephen, Sir George. *Anti-Slavery Recollections in a Series of Letters Addressed to Mrs. Beecher Stowe, Written by Sir George Stephen at Her Request*. 2d ed. London: Cass, 1971.

Sturge, Joseph and Thomas Harvey. *The West Indies in 1837* . . . . London: Hamilton, Adams, 1838.

Sunstein, Emily. *A Different Face: The Life of Mary Wollstonecraft*. New York: Harper & Row, 1975.

Sypher, Wylie. "The West-Indian as a 'Character' in the Eighteenth Century." *Studies in Philology* 36, no. 3 (July 1939): 503–20.

Thome, James A. and J. Horace Kimball. *Emancipation in the West Indies*. New York: Anti-Slavery Society, 1838.

Tiffin, Helen. "Mirror and Mask: Colonial Motifs in the Novels of Jean Rhys." *World Literature Written in English* 17 (1978): 328–41.

Todd, Janet, ed. *A Wollstonecraft Anthology*. New York: Columbia University Press, 1990.

Todorov, Tzvetan. *The Conquest of America: A Question of the Other*. Translated by Richard Howard. New York: Harper & Row, 1984.

Tomalin, Claire. *The Life and Death of Mary Wollstonecraft.* New York: Harcourt Brace Jovanovich, 1974.

Turner, Mary. *Slaves & Missionaries: The Disintegration of Jamaican Slave Society, 1787–1834.* Urbana: University of Illinois Press, 1982.

Walvin, James. *The Black Presence: A Documentary History of the Negro in England, 1555–1860.* New York: Schocken, 1971.

Wardle, Ralph M. *Mary Wollstonecraft: A Critical Biography.* Lincoln: University of Nebraska Press, 1966.

———, ed. *Collected Letters of Mary Wollstonecraft.* Ithaca: Cornell University Press, 1979.

Willcox, William B. *The Age of Aristocracy, 1688 to 1830.* 2d ed. Lexington, Mass.: Heath, 1971.

Williams, Eric. *Capitalism and Slavery.* 1944. Reprint, New York: Capricorn, 1966.

Williams, Raymond. *The Country and the City.* New York: Oxford University Press, 1973.

Wilson, Ellen Gibson. *The Loyal Blacks.* New York: Putnam, 1976.

Wollstonecraft, Mary. *Mary* and *The Wrongs of Woman.* 1788. Reprint, edited and introduced by Gary Kelly. London: Oxford University Press, 1976.

———. *The Female Reader . . . .* London: Johnson, 1789.

———. *A Vindication of the Rights of Men . . . .* 2d ed. London: Johnson, 1790.

———. *A Vindication of the Rights of Woman.* 1792. 2d ed. edited by Carol H. Poston. New York: W. W. Norton, 1988.

———. *The Wrongs of Woman.* 1798. Reprint, edited and introduced by Gary Kelly. London: Oxford University Press, 1976.

Wyndham, Francis and Diana Melly, eds. *Jean Rhys Letters, 1931–1966.* London: Andre Deutsch, 1984.

Yeazell, Ruth Bernard. "The Boundaries of Mansfield Park." *Representations* 6 (Spring 1984): 133–52.

Zuill, William. *Bermuda Sampler, 1815–1850 . . . .* Bermuda: 1937. Reprint, Suffolk, England: Richard Clay, n.d.

Index

171

Index

Index

Index

CPSIA information can be obtained
at www.ICGtesting.com
Printed in the USA
JSHW041944121220
10200JS00006B/102

9 780231 082235